**Looking at Geography 3**

# Looking at Britain

**Jean and David Gadsby**

A and C Black · London

General editor: R J Unstead

1 Looking at Other Children
2 Looking at Everyday Things
3 Looking at Britain
4 Looking at the World Today
5 Looking at Scotland
6 Looking at Wales

Books 1–4 are also published in a complete one-volume edition called *Looking at the World*

The authors are grateful to the following for their help with specific chapters of this book: Gwynneth Ashby (*Glass, Pottery* and *Fishing*); Association of Agriculture and Vivien Young (*Farming*); BL Components (*Making cars*); BP Chemicals Ltd (*Chemicals*); BP Oil Ltd (*Oil refining*); British Aerospace (*Building aircraft*); British Gas (*Natural gas and oil*); British Shipbuilders (*Shipbuilding*); British Steel (*Iron and steel*); Central Electricity Generating Board (*Electrical power*); Courtaulds (*Clothing*); Tony Durham (*Electronics and computers*); Isabel Harris (*Transport, Communications*); Imperial Chemical Industries Ltd (*Plastics and man-made fibres*); National Coal Board (*Coal*); Port of London Authority (*Changing Britain*). They would also like to thank Burberrys Ltd, Allen W Cotton, Christopher Dench and J F Richards for help in obtaining illustrations.

**Photographs**
Abacus Municipal Ltd 58b; Aerofilms Ltd 42a, 43b, 93a; Arundel Associates (Plastics) Ltd 69b; Association of Agriculture 62a, 63a and b, 66a and b; Margaret Baker 40a and c, 41a and b, 43c, 61b, 71a, 72b, 73a, 80a and b; Barnaby's Picture Library 12a, 29a, 45a and c, 46a, b, c and d, 47a, b and c, 56a and b, 57a, 58a, 59b, 63c, 65a, 67a, 73b, 75b and c, 76b, 82a and c; *Brentwood Gazette* 45b; BBC Photographs 53b; BL Components Ltd 25b and c; BP Oil Ltd 9b and c, 13; BP Chemicals Ltd 15a, b and c; British Aerospace 20a, 29b and c; British Airways 3, 86a, b, c and d, 87a; British Rail 19b, 82b, 83b and c, 84a, b and c, 85a, b and c; British Shipbuilders 27a and b, 28a and b; British Steel 21a and b, 22a and b, 23a, 24b and c; British Sugar Bureau 67b; British Waterways Board 89a; Camera Press 60b; J Allan Cash Ltd 57c, 61a; Central Electricity Generating Board 10, 11a, b and d; Courtaulds Ltd 20c, 35a, b and c, 37b, 38a, b and c, 39a; Covent Garden Market Authority 70b; Christopher Dench 72c; Drake & Fletcher Ltd 71b; Ford Motor Company Ltd 25a; R J Fullwood & Bland Ltd 59a; Walter Fussey & Son 78b, 79c; Glass Manufacturers' Federation 32a; Glasgow Passenger Executive 83a; *The Grower* 70a; Handford Photography 93b; Kenneth Howells (PR) Associates 88a; International Wool Secretariat 36a and b, 37a, 39b and c, 40b; John Laing Services Ltd 28c; Land Settlement Association 68, 69a; Elsa Mayo 70c; Metal Closures Thermoplastics Ltd 16a, b and c, 17b and c; Milk Marketing Board 58c; MK Electric Ltd 17a; National Coal Board 7b and c, 8a, b and c; Ann Nichols 74a and b; PBP International Picture Library 77b, 79a; Pilkington Brothers Ltd 31a; Plessey Semiconductors Ltd 18, 19a; P&O Ferries 88b; Port of London Authority 94a and b, 95a, b and c; Post Office 19c, 20b, 90a, b and c, 91a, b and c, 92a, b and c; Potato Marketing Board 64a and c, 65a; Safety Representatives Publications Ltd 89b; F A Standen & Sons (Engineering) Ltd 67c; Storey Brothers and Company Ltd 16d; Thames Water Authority 48a, 49a, b and c, 50a and b; John Topham Picture Library 57b; Unigate Dairies Ltd 60a; Unimation (Europe) Ltd 26b; University of Dundee Satellite Receiving Station 53a; University of Edinburgh School of Engineering Science 12c; Vauxhall Motors Ltd 26a; Josiah Wedgwood and Sons Ltd 1, 33a and b, 34a, b and c; White Fish Authority 78d, 80c; Ralph Wright 87b; Young's Seafoods Ltd 79b

Drawings Brian L Ainsworth. The Ordnance Survey 1:1250 map on page 42, the 1:2500 map on page 43 and the 1:10000 map on page 44 were reproduced with the permission of The Controller of Her Majesty's Stationery Office, Crown Copyright Reserved.

Designed by Ann Samuel

*All rights reserved. No part of this publication may be reproduced, stored in any retrieval system, or transmitted, in any form or by any means, electronic, mechanical, photocopying, recording or otherwise, without the prior permission of A & C Black (Publishers) Ltd*

Fourth edition 1980
Copyright © A & C Black (Publishers) Ltd, 35 Bedford Row, London WC1R 4JH

Printed and bound in Great Britain by Hazell Watson & Viney Ltd, Aylesbury, Bucks

**British Library Cataloguing in Publication Data**
Gadsby, Jean
　Looking at Britain.–4th ed.–
　(Looking at geography; book 3).
　1. Great Britain–Description and travel
　–1971–
　I. Title　II. Gadsby, David　III. Series
　914.1　　　DA632

ISBN 0–7136–1954–6
ISBN 0–7136–1852–3 (non-net)

# Contents

About this book  5
Power for our homes and factories  6
   Fossil fuels  6
   Coal  7
   Natural gas and oil  9
   Electrical power  10
   Finding other sources of power  12
Oil  13
   Oil refining  13
   Chemicals  14
   Plastics and man-made fibres  16
Electronics and computers  18
Iron and steel  21
   Making cars  25
   Shipbuilding  27
   Civil engineering and construction  28
   Using other metals and alloys: building aircraft  29
Glass  31
Pottery  33
Clothing  35
Maps, scales and contours  41

A town and its services  45
   Refuse  47
   Water  48
Day, night and the seasons  51
Britain's weather  53
Farming  56
   A dairy farm in the West Country  57
   A farm in the Yorkshire Dales  61
   An arable farm in Lincolnshire  64
   Market gardening  68
   Fruit farming in Kent  71
   British farming today  75
Fishing  76
Transport  81
   Road  82
   Rail  83
   Air  86
   Crossing the Channel and the North Sea  88
   Transport and the environment  89
Communications  90
   Post  90
   Telecommunications  91
Changing Britain  93
Index  96

Key
National border
High land
Capital city
City
River
Scale
0 km
100 km
N
SHETLAND ISLANDS
ORKNEY ISLANDS
Inverness
Aberdeen
SCOTLAND
Dundee
Perth
Glasgow
Edinburgh
Clyde
NORTHERN IRELAND
Belfast
Newcastle-upon-Tyne
Tyne
Wear
LAKE DISTRICT
Tees
Middlesbrough
YORKSHIRE DALES
ISLE OF MAN
LANCASHIRE
Leeds
Hull
Bradford
Doncaster
Liverpool
Manchester
Sheffield
Mersey
LINCOLNSHIRE
REPUBLIC OF IRELAND
Derby
Stoke-on -Trent
Nottingham
STAFFORDSHIRE
Leicester
Norwich
Birmingham
Coventry
Cambridge
ENGLAND
Ipswich
WALES
Harwich
Oxford
Swansea
Cardiff
Tilbury
Bristol
Thames
London
KENT
Dover
SOMERSET
EAST SUSSEX
Southampton
Portsmouth
DEVON
DORSET
ISLE OF WIGHT
Plymouth
CORNWALL

# About this book

This book is about life in Britain and about the ways its people earn their livings. Some people make goods which can be sold in shops at home or overseas. A few produce food or catch fish. Many work in service industries which supply our homes and factories with light, heat and power, or which provide transport for people and goods. Others are nurses, teachers, firemen, police, shop and office workers, postmen and weather forecasters. They all do important jobs.

As well as telling you about people and their work, this book also shows you how maps are made and tells you about the weather and the seasons.

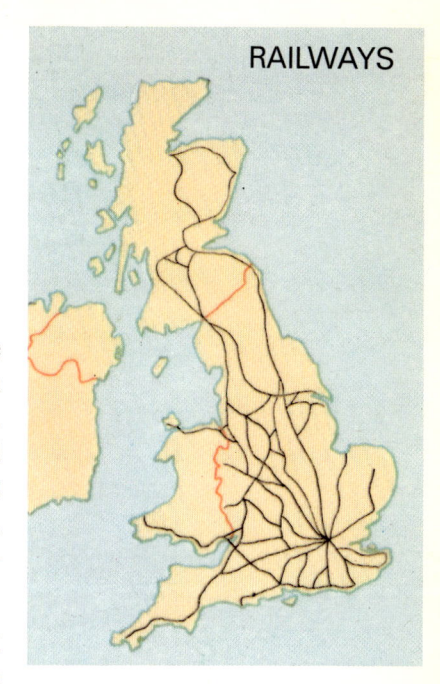

## Britain

On the facing page you can see a map of Britain. It shows you the areas of high land (chiefly in the north and west) and the wide expanse of low land (in the south and east). You can see how the rivers rise in the hills and flow across the lower land to the sea.

The map also shows the big cities of Britain, some of the towns, and the counties and districts that are mentioned in the book. You will need to look at this map while you are reading this book.

In the small maps on this page you can see the main roads and railways of Britain. If you compare these maps with the big one, you can see why their builders chose the routes they did.

# Power for our homes and factories

**How coal was formed over millions of years**

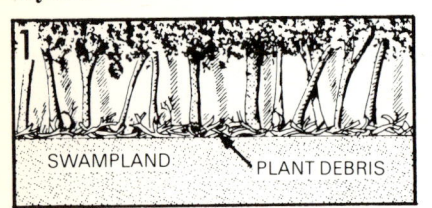

*Dead plants decay and form peat*

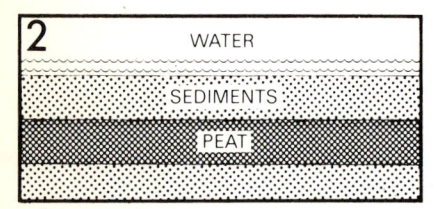

*Mud and sand settle on top of the peat*

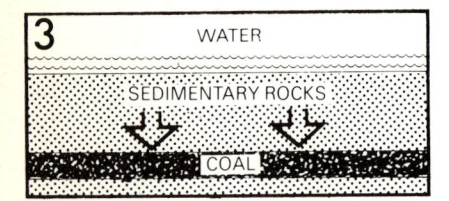

*The mud and sand harden into rocks which press down on the peat, turning it into coal*

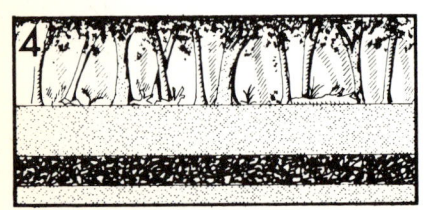

*Coal lies under the ground*

For thousands of years the power needed to do heavy work was provided by the muscles of men and of animals. Power for smelting metals or for firing pottery was produced by burning wood. Water and wind power were used for turning mills and for driving ships. But the wind could drop or the water in the mill stream could freeze or dry up. And, as forests were cut down, wood for fuel grew scarce.

When people discovered how to use coal as a fuel, and when they invented a coal-burning steam engine, work could be done in factories—more work than people could do on their own. In Britain, the first country in the world to become an industrial nation, large manufacturing areas grew up around the coalfields.

## Fossil fuels

Coal was the first of the "fossil fuels" to be used. The others are natural gas and oil.

Coal is called a fossil fuel because it is the fossil remains of trees and plants which lived millions of years ago. The trees were buried under mud, sand and rock, instead of rotting away completely, as normally happens. They were preserved deep underground and formed a layer of coal.

Oil and gas are also called fossil fuels because they too were formed millions of years ago—from the decaying bodies of sea creatures. But these were not really fossilized; they underwent a complete change into crude oil or natural gas. Sometimes this oil or gas was trapped in rock cavities. It is this trapped oil or gas which the oil companies look for in their exploration.

*Power for our homes and factories*

## Coal

Britain's coal-mining industry is one of the biggest in Europe. Work that used to be done by men with picks and shovels is now done by machines which move along the coal seams under the ground, cutting the coal and loading it automatically on to conveyors.

At most of Britain's mines the coal is very deep underground and has to be lifted up vertical shafts to the surface.

At some mines the coal is not far below the surface and can be brought out up a long sloping tunnel called a "drift". At Longannet in Scotland the coal is carried on the world's longest conveyor system straight to one of Britain's largest power stations which generates enough electricity to supply the needs of Edinburgh and Glasgow.

At some mines near the coast coal is mined from coal seams lying under the seabed several kilometres offshore.

The world's biggest underground mine is being built at Selby in Yorkshire to work the recently discovered Selby coalfield. Great care is being taken to protect the landscape and the town of Selby, with its ancient church, from damage.

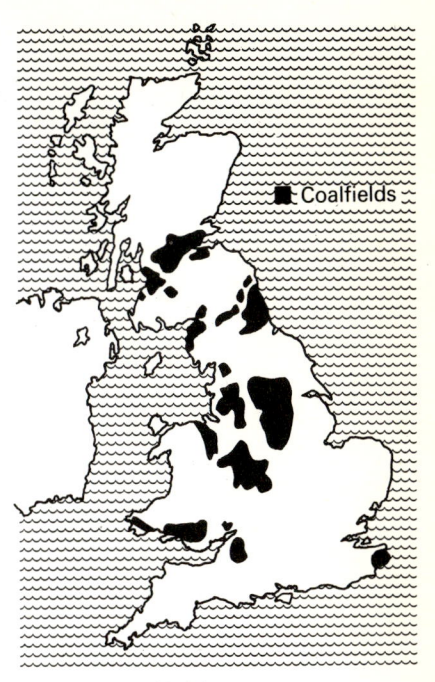

*Britain's coalfields*

*The conveyor in a drift mine*

*A giant machine which cuts coal and loads it on to a conveyor*

*Coal from Lea Hall colliery in Staffordshire is fed direct to Rugeley power station. (You can see the colliery winding gear and the power station cooling towers)*

Sometimes coal lies just beneath the surface and can be dug out without going underground. This is called *opencast mining*. Huge mechanical excavators and other machines are used to scoop off the topsoil and take out the coal. Then the topsoil is replaced and the land is restored to its original use. When derelict land is used for opencast mining, it is afterwards improved so that it can be used for a park or something else useful to the community.

At the moment over 75 per cent of Britain's coal goes to power stations and as coke to the steel industry (see page 21). About nine per cent is used for heating homes. The rest goes to industry, for export and for use as a raw material in making chemicals (see page 14).

Britain's coalfields could supply coal for at least three hundred years, long after our oil and natural gas have run out. A great deal of research is being done to find new ways of using coal. Coal could be made into "substitute natural gas" for cooking and heating; into liquid fuels such as petrol and diesel fuel for vehicles and aviation fuel; and into chemicals.

*The control room for the machines that wash and sort the coal*

*An opencast mine with a dragline excavator at work*

*Power for our homes and factories*

## Natural gas and oil

Britain has only recently become a gas-producing and oil-producing country. Small oil fields had been found on the mainland of Britain. But not until the 1960s did oil companies begin to explore the North Sea.

The first worthwhile gas field was found in 1965 and other gas finds soon followed. By 1967 the first North Sea gas was being fed into the national grid—nearly 5000 kilometres of pipeline that carries gas all over Great Britain. By 1977 the gas-burning equipment of Great Britain had been converted to burn natural gas (methane) instead of town gas made from coal or oil. Only Northern Ireland continued to burn town gas made from oil.

Gas-fired central heating became very popular and many industries began to use gas instead of electricity or oil.

The first major North Sea oil field was found in October 1970 and the first oil from a production well in the British sector of the North Sea came ashore in September 1975. Oil production increased rapidly so that by 1980 it was about equal to the amount used in Britain each year.

The two main United Kingdom fields are the Forties, east of Aberdeen, and Brent, north-east of the Shetlands. Other areas of the sea around Britain are being explored in the hope of finding further oil fields.

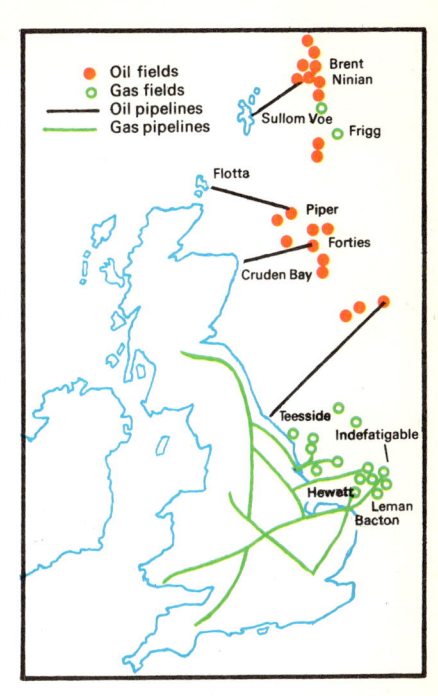

*Oil and gas fields in the North Sea*

*An oilman prepares a diving bell for work near the surface*

*An oil production platform in the Forties field*

*Power for our homes and factories*

## Electrical power

One of the power sources we use most in our daily lives is electricity. Electric power can be generated in one place and used many kilometres away. A network of cables, the National Grid, enables electricity to be distributed throughout the country and even to be exchanged with other countries.

When a cyclist switches on his dynamo, it converts the power or energy of his muscles into electricity for the bicycle lamp. In a similar way, in a power station, the power used to make a turbine revolve is converted into an electric current by a generator.

### Steam power stations

Most power stations use steam to turn the turbines. Nearly all the power stations use one type of fuel (coal, oil, natural gas or nuclear), although a small number can burn more than one fuel. Some are built in places where there is a good supply of fuel, for instance, coal at Longannet or natural gas coming ashore from the Brent oil field at Peterhead in Scotland.

In power stations using coal, oil or gas these fuels are burnt to heat the water which is turned into steam. The steam is then forced through the turbines.

*A coal-fired power station near Nottingham*

*(Left) A nuclear power station in Suffolk. (Below) A giant refuelling machine about to put nuclear fuel into the reactor below the floor*

Nuclear power stations are different. You have heard of the terrible force of an atomic bomb. This is the result of what is called a *nuclear reaction*. In a nuclear power station a very carefully controlled nuclear reaction takes place inside the reactor core and the enormous heat given off during the reaction is used to heat either gas or water. This in turn is used to heat the water which produces steam to power the turbines.

## Hydro-electric power

In Scotland and Wales, where there is a high annual rainfall, water power can be used to turn the turbines of power stations. This is called hydro-electric power (*hydro* means water). Engineers build a dam across a valley so that water from streams and rivers forms a lake behind the dam. From the lake the water is fed down tunnels and the force of the water turns the turbines in the power station below the dam.

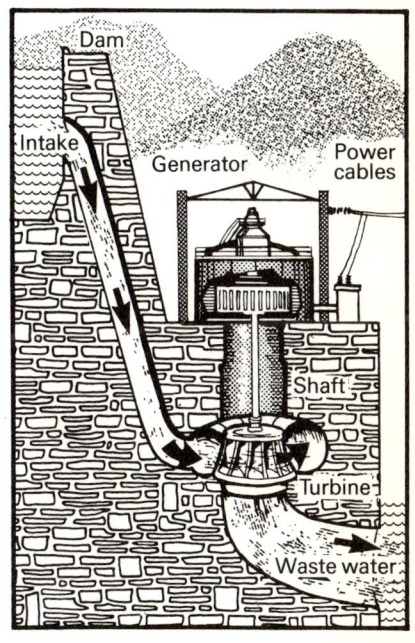

*In a hydro-electric scheme the force of the water rushing down the tunnels turns the turbines. (Left) A hydro-electric station in Wales. The dam can be seen above the station*

C11

*Power for our homes and factories*

## Finding other sources of power

During the 1970s people began to realize that the world's resources of fossil fuels would not last for ever, and that they should use these fuels sparingly and look for other sources of power.

Already *solar energy* (from the rays of the sun) is being used to heat some houses. Scientists and engineers are exploring many other ideas. Can the gas hydrogen be used safely as a fuel? Are ships with sails as well as engines a way of saving fuel? Can the waves of the sea or the tides be used to generate electricity? Is it possible to use heat from deep below the earth's surface to generate electricity or to supply hot water for heating?

A great deal of time and money will have to be spent on research before any of these ideas can be tried out, even on a small scale. In the meantime the government is trying to persuade people to save energy by insulating their homes, buying cars with smaller engines and using trains and buses instead of private cars.

*A house heated by solar energy*

*(Left) An idea for a rocking-float, about the size of a supertanker. The movement of the float would generate electricity inside the central core (Right) Testing a rocking-float or duck in the tank of an engineering laboratory at Edinburgh University*

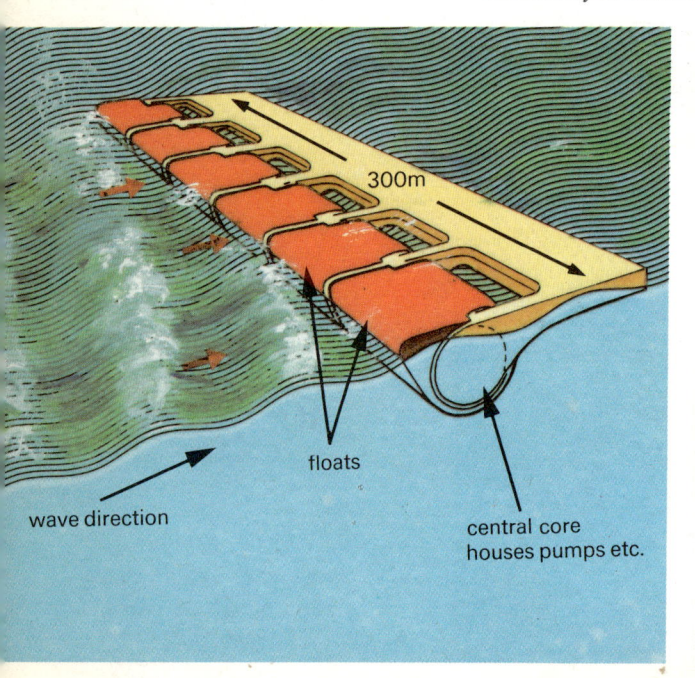

# Oil

## Oil refining

The crude oil from the North Sea or from oil fields abroad cannot be used as it is, for it is a mixture of different types of oil. Imagine a mixture of petrol, paraffin, diesel oil and some of the thick tar which sometimes pollutes our beaches. It is the job of the oil refinery to sort out these different types of oil so that each can be used for the purpose for which it is most suited.

Have you noticed how the few drops of petrol which drip on to the ground at a filling station evaporate or turn to gas almost at once? But a paraffin spill takes much longer to disappear? This is because petrol and paraffin turn to gas or boil at different temperatures. The various types of oil contained in crude oil all have different boiling points and this is used as a means of separating them.

*Grangemouth oil refinery in Stirlingshire*

## Oil

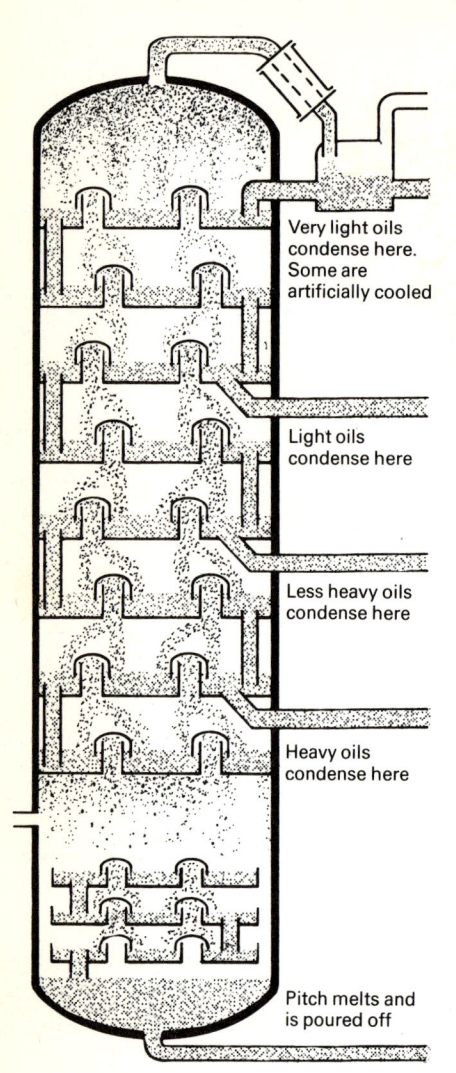

At the refinery the crude oil is heated to 300 °C. Most of it turns to gas and passes into a distillation column, a tower built in stages, with a bubble cap tray at each stage.

Trays near the bottom of the column, where the temperature is around 280 °C, fill with heavy diesel oil which is piped off. A little further up the column the trays are cooler and kerosine (or paraffin) collects. As each tray in the column is cooler than the one below, it collects a different type of oil.

At the very top of the column the tray is cool enough to liquefy light gasoline or petrol. The only gases left are those which must be frozen in order to become liquid and these are piped away from the top of the column.

The thick liquid which did not turn to gas in this process is left at the bottom of the column. This has to be heated at low pressure before it will boil and produce heavy fuel oil for heating, generating electricity and making lubricating oils. The bitumen which is left over from this is used for surfacing roads and making roofing felt.

The refinery can increase the yield of petrol from a crude oil by "cracking" heavy fuel oil to produce petrol.

Besides producing a wide range of fuels, oils and gases which are sold direct to the public and to industry, oil refineries also produce raw materials or *feedstocks* for other industries, particularly the chemical industry.

*A distillation column. Heated crude oil passes into the column near the bottom*

Very light oils condense here. Some are artificially cooled

Light oils condense here

Less heavy oils condense here

Heavy oils condense here

Pitch melts and is poured off

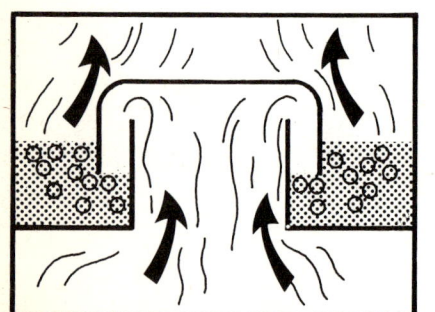

*How the bubble cap tray works*

## Chemicals

Britain has one of the largest chemical industries in Europe. It has specialized branches which produce medicines, vaccines, anaesthetics, photographic chemicals, fertilizers, soaps and cosmetics. Much of its production is of chemicals that other manufacturers can use in their industries. Most of these are based on feedstocks made from oil, gas and coal.

We have seen how an oil refinery can change one type of oil into another. In the chemical industry this process is carried still further.

*(Left) Polymers, the basic materials used in making plastics and man-made fibres, are made in these vessels*

Most of the processes are long and complicated. The feedstock may be mixed with other chemicals, heated, compressed or pass through a vacuum. At each stage it changes.

The products of the chemical industry go to manufacturers who make plastics and man-made fibres, detergents, paints, adhesives, agricultural chemicals and many other things for use in industry and in our daily lives.

*Checking that a chemical plant has not polluted a river*

*Loading a tanker with hydrochloric acid*

# Electronics and computers

Every day we use radios, television sets, tape recorders, record players. All are made by the electronics industry. Many other things we do need electronics.

Ships and aircraft find their way with the help of radar. Satellites and spacecraft are packed with electronics. Communications satellites relay telephone calls and television pictures between the continents. Other satellites watch the clouds from above and help us forecast the weather.

All kinds of machines have electronics built into them as part of their control systems. Even machines you might not think were electronic, such as cars, cameras or washing machines, may have electronic parts and mechanisms inside them.

The products of the electronics industry are complicated and sometimes expensive, but they do not require very large amounts of raw materials. Many electronics factories are in south-east England. North-west England, the West Midlands and Scotland are also important electronic manufacturing areas.

*A "chip". It contains 1000 components and can be used in a colour television set or for controlling the speed of an electric motor*

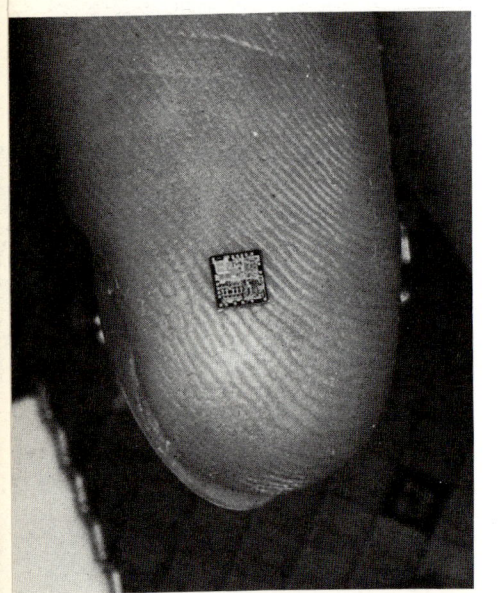

## Transistors and "chips"

Many electronics factories make *components* which can be assembled into electronic equipment. The *transistor* is an important type of component. If you could look inside a television set, you would see that it is built of components of many types, including transistors.

Another important type of component is the *integrated circuit*. You need a microscope to see how complicated it is inside. The heart of the integrated circuit is a tiny piece of silicon about the size of a matchhead, known as a *chip*. (Silicon is a substance found in sand, flint and many forms of rock.) A single integrated circuit can do a job which once would have required hundreds or thousands of components. They make it possible to fit complicated electronic equipment into a very small space. Electronic watches and pocket calculators use integrated circuits.

*Electronics and computers*

## Microprocessors

Some chips do very specialized jobs. But one type, the *microprocessor*, can be used for many different purposes. To make it work it has to be given instructions. Microprocessors can control industrial machinery, office equipment, scientific instruments and such familiar machines as petrol pumps and washing machines. Computers built with microprocessors are smaller and cheaper than ever before.

*A toy train controlled by an electronic remote-control device*

## Computers

The computing industry started only in the late 1940s, but it has grown very fast. Britain has one of the few companies outside the United States that sell large computers to the world. In addition there are several firms that make smaller computers and many firms make equipment to be connected to computers.

## Hardware and software

What a computer can do does not only depend on the machinery itself. Equally important are the *programs* (note how the word is spelt in the computer world). A program is a list of instructions in a code or language that the computer can obey. With one program a computer could land a spacecraft; with others the same computer could print a telephone directory or teach someone French.

*This is British Rail's freight-services computer (see page 85). The information it uses is stored on plastic discs, which look like long-playing records*

*The computer operator "talks" to a computer by typing out messages on a keyboard. The computer's reply appears on the screen. This computer controls British Airways' freight services*

*A fully automated machine for drilling holes and riveting*

*A bank cashier contacts a central computer for information about a customer's account*

*A textile designer uses a computer to work out new patterns and colour combinations*

The products of the computing industry are of two kinds. Actual machinery is known as *hardware*. Programs are known as *software*. The British software industry has a good reputation in the world.

The computer has spread to most walks of life. Here are just a few examples. A large chemical plant is kept operating efficiently and safely by a few workers with the help of a computer. In an engineering factory an engineer sits at a computer screen to design a gearbox. The machine that cuts the gears out of metal does not need to be controlled by hand; it is controlled by a paper tape prepared by the computer. In a bank a central computer keeps customers' accounts for many local branches.

**Automation**

Computers are part of the process called *automation*. More and more of the work formerly done by human brains is now being done by machine.

Not everyone sees this as a good thing. A skilled worker who has spent many years learning a trade does not like to see his or her job taken over by a computer. On the other hand computers have created many new jobs which did not exist before.

Some people expect that automation will bring an age of leisure in which people have to work only a few hours each week. Others fear that automation will leave large numbers of people with nothing to do and no way of earning money, while only a lucky few have jobs. Whichever happens, automation will surely have a big effect on the way we live and work in years to come.

# Iron and steel

## Making iron and steel

Britain was the first country to make iron and steel on a large scale and for many years British steel was exported all over the world. Now many countries which used to buy steel from Britain have their own steelworks, so the demand for British steel has grown less.

Britain's steelmakers are continually trying to find ways of making steel products of the highest quality. Out-of-date works are being modernized or shut down and important changes are taking place in the industry.

Some steel (about 30 per cent) is made by melting steel scrap in electric arc furnaces. But more than half the steel produced in Britain is made at steelworks which carry out all the processes to change iron ore (a rock found beneath the ground) into steel products which can be used by industry.

A big modern steelworks needs a deep-water port so that its supplies of iron ore from overseas can be delivered directly to the works. It needs to be linked to a railway so that coal and limestone can be brought to the works and so that steel products can be taken to customers (see page 85). It has coke ovens in which coal is made into coke (coke is an essential material for transforming iron ore into iron in the blast furnace).

*Iron ore from overseas being unloaded from a bulk carrier*

*A modern steelworks which makes iron and then converts it to steel*

*Iron and steel*

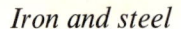

## Making iron

Iron ore is made up of iron and oxygen. Smelting splits it into molten iron and gases. This is done in a steel tower called a blast furnace. (The biggest blast furnace is 87 metres high and 14 metres in diameter.) It is lined with fire-resistant bricks. At the bottom is a hearth with a fiercely burning fire.

The iron ore is mixed with coke and limestone and fed in at the top. Blasts of very hot air and fuel oil from nozzles round the lower part of the furnace raise the temperature to white heat.

Carbon from the coke combines with the oxygen in the iron ore to form gas, leaving molten iron. (Carbon is a substance found in most fuels—coal, wood, oil. Coke has a very high carbon content.)

Unwanted ashes and impurities fuse (combine) with the limestone to make molten slag which floats on top of the iron. The slag and the iron are let out of the furnace in two separate streams.

The molten iron is carried in huge ladles on railway trucks to the steel-making plant.

*Materials for the furnace being mixed by a machine*

*In these huge ovens coke is made from coal*

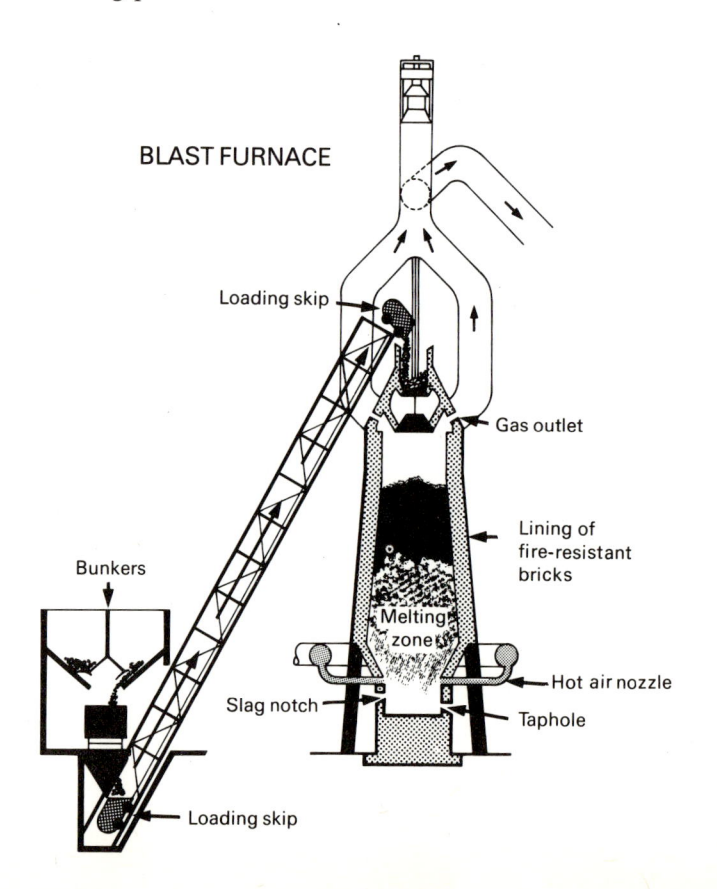

**BLAST FURNACE**

- Loading skip
- Gas outlet
- Lining of fire-resistant bricks
- Melting zone
- Bunkers
- Hot air nozzle
- Slag notch
- Taphole
- Loading skip

*Iron and steel*

## Making steel

The iron produced by a blast furnace is not pure. It contains carbon from the coke and other impurities. If it were used as it is, it would break easily. The process of steel-making removes some of this carbon, leaving a material which is stronger than iron and which can bend without breaking.

The amount of carbon left in the steel decides what kind of steel it is going to be. For instance, "mild" steel, which is used for steel sheet and is very flexible, contains less carbon than "high carbon" steel which is used for drills, files and other tools.

Iron is made into steel in a *converter*, a huge pear-shaped pot, lined with fire-resistant material, which can be tipped on its side for loading and emptying. It is charged or loaded with steel scrap and then with molten iron.

A jet of oxygen, moving at supersonic speed, is directed on to the molten iron and scrap. Then lime is added; this fuses with the impurities to make slag. The unwanted carbon combines with the oxygen, leaving molten steel.

*"Charging" or loading the converter with hot metal (molten iron from the blast furnace)*

*The stages of making steel from iron*

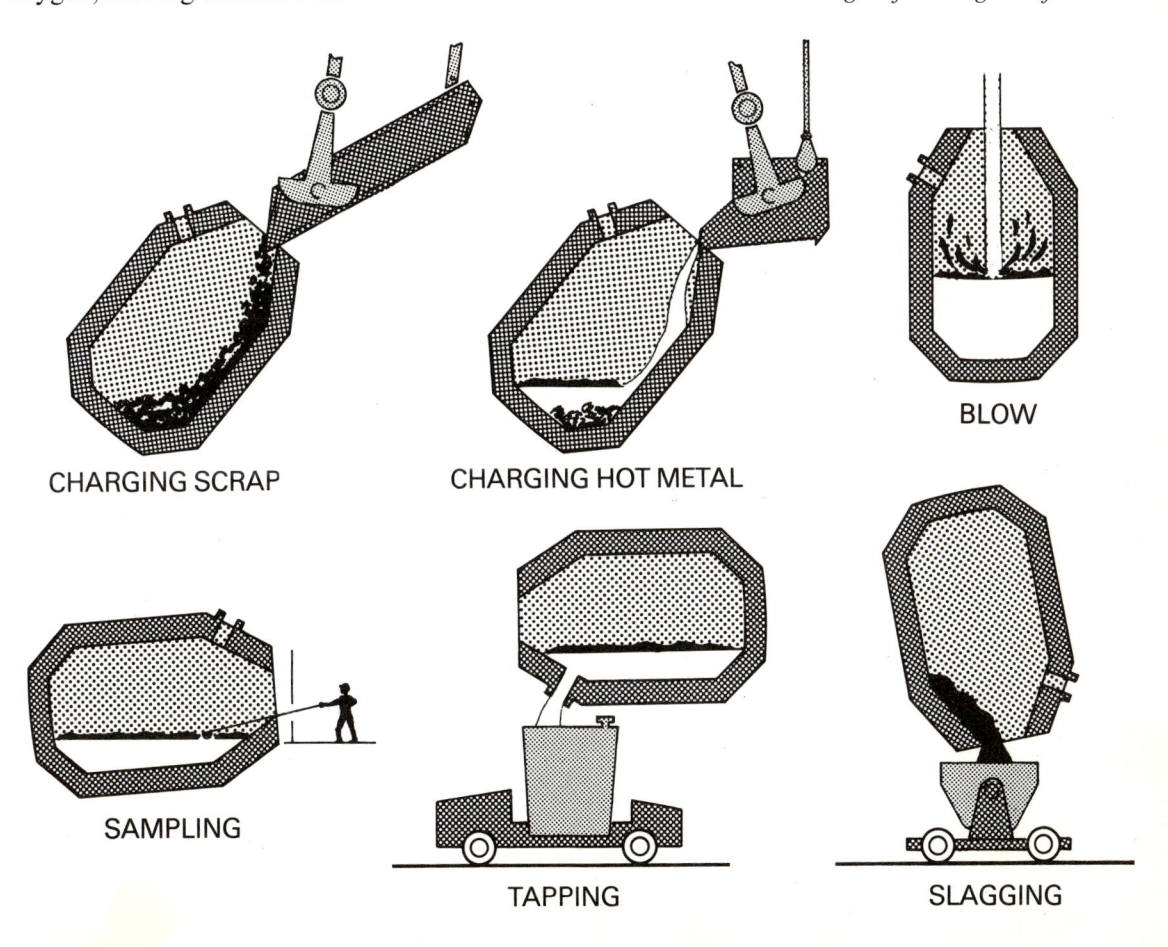

CHARGING SCRAP

CHARGING HOT METAL

BLOW

SAMPLING

TAPPING

SLAGGING

*Iron and steel*

## CONTINUOUS CASTING

- Molten steel
- Water-cooled mould
- Spray cooling chamber
- Withdrawal rolls
- Bending roller
- Straightener rolls
- Torch cutter

This steel is then usually cast into wedge-shaped blocks called *ingots*. These are then rolled into a variety of "semi-finished" shapes in rolling mills. Some ingots are forged by steam-powered hammers to form heavy engine parts, or pressed in huge presses to make turbine rotors for power stations and ships.

A more modern process for forming "semi-finished" steel is the continuous-casting machine. In this process the molten metal is poured into a water-cooled mould and cools and hardens as it reaches the bottom. The first metal to reach the bottom solidifies on to a "dummy bar" which is slowly pulled out of the mould, taking the metal with it. In this way molten metal is poured in at one end of the machine and partly solidified metal is drawn out at the other in a continuous process. The slab of steel produced is then cut into lengths and cooled.

While semi-finished steel is still red-hot and soft, it has to be rolled to make it strong and to get rid of any weak spots. Then it passes through further rolling mills which give it its final shape. One set of rolls produces rails or sections (see page 27), another rods for wire-making. Others roll the steel into plates or thin strip such as is used for making motor-car bodies.

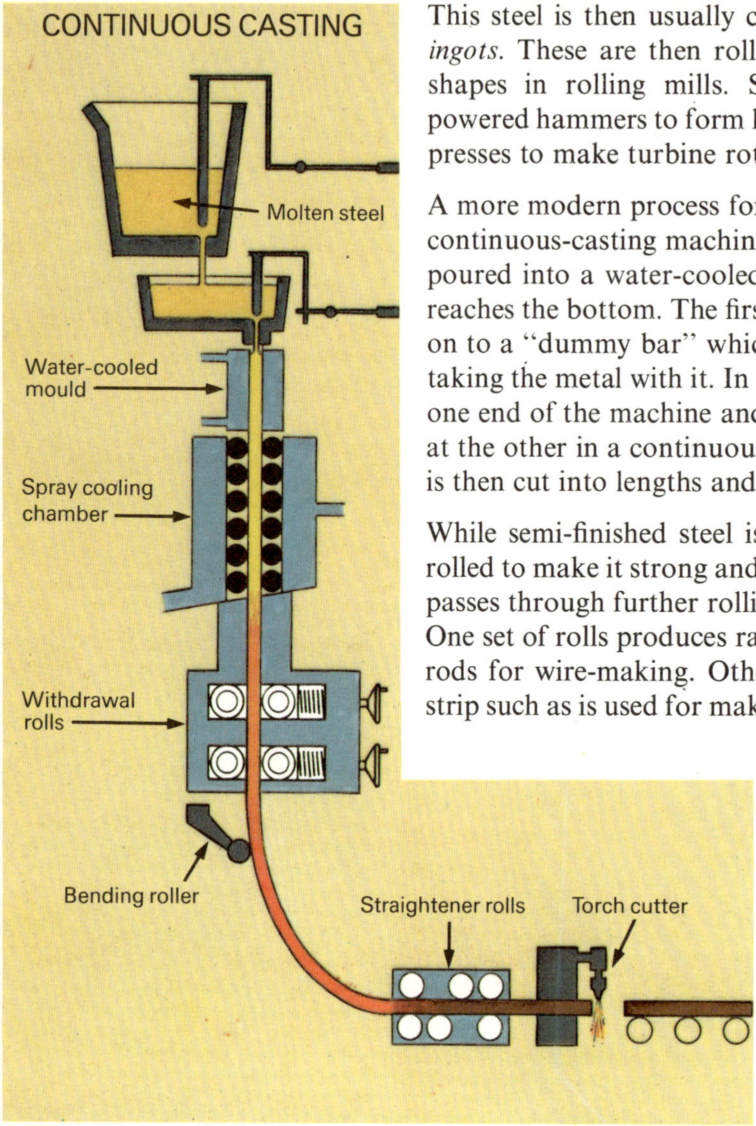

*Partly solidified steel leaving the continuous-casting machine*

*(Below) Roll of steel strip (Above) Casting ingots*

*Iron and steel*

# Using iron and steel

## Making cars

A car factory is a good place to see iron and steel being used for they form at least 70 per cent of the materials used.

A car is a large and complicated piece of machinery which needs to be produced in large numbers (so that it can be made more cheaply). Cars are made in big factories by mass-production methods. This means that each worker does only one small part of the work on each car.

The part of the car he works on is brought to his work station by a conveyor. He carries out his job and the conveyor moves on to the next man or to the next automatic machine. In modern car factories machines are linked together to carry out several jobs, one after another, without human help.

There are several assembly lines in each factory. One long one builds up the engine. Another fits together the working parts— the engine, gearbox, transmission, wheels and axles. This line meets another, a high-level one, from which the car bodies are hanging. The body and the working parts are bolted together and the finished car can be driven away from the end of the assembly line.

*Fitting the body of a car together from panels of pressed steel*

## Cast iron

Many of a car's large heavy working parts are cast from iron— for instance, the cylinder block which is the heavy iron casing of the engine. When the cylinder block is cast, it is given some crude shaping and holes are made so that water can pass through to cool the engine. But very accurate work is needed to make the cylinders in which the pistons move up and down. These are made by machine tools which cut away the metal and produce a cylinder to the exact size needed.

*The body of the car is lowered on to the engine and axles*

*A factory makes its own stamps for pressing out car body parts*

*Car body panels which have been shaped on a giant press*

*The most up-to-date car factories have robot assembly lines. Each robot does a different job.*

## Steel sheet

The body of the car is made from steel sheet. Huge presses stamp out and force the steel into the special shapes needed for the roof, boot, bonnet, wings, floor panel and doors. Steel sheet is very thin, so it needs to be strengthened. The outside of a car door is an almost flat sheet of steel fastened to a framework which has also been pressed out of sheet.

The pieces that make up the car body are fastened together by spot welding. At each spot where a join is to be made, an electric current is passed through the steel. This makes it so hot that the steel actually melts in that spot and joins or fuses together. Several thousand welds are needed for each car and these can be done by robot welding machines, each one carrying out the welds on one part of the body.

## Forged steel

Heavy moving parts of the engine, such as the crankshaft, are forged from steel bars. These are heated until they are soft enough to be hammered or pressed into shape. Then they too are given their final shaping by machine tools.

Britain's large car factories are found in the West Midlands (at Coventry and Birmingham), in southern England (at Oxford, Luton and Dagenham), in Merseyside and Lancashire and in Scotland.

*Iron and steel*

## Shipbuilding

Shipbuilders are important users of steel and shipyards tend to be sited conveniently for the delivery of steel. The two most important ship-building areas in Britain are the mouths of the rivers Tyne, Wear and Tees in north-east England and Clydeside in Scotland. Britain's biggest single shipyard is in Belfast.

Britain used to be the world's leading shipbuilding country but now many other countries are building ships. Some of Britain's shipyards and the companies that supply them with equipment have switched their skills to working for the North Sea oil industry, building production platforms, drilling barges and other installations.

### Steel plates

The hull of a ship is built up of steel plates stiffened with "sections". A section is a steel bar which has been rolled to a particular shape—its cross-section may be a T or an L, for instance.

The steel plates are cut to shape by oxy-acetylene cutters. These may be guided by a computer which has been programmed with the design of the ship and automatically cuts the plates to the sizes needed. The plates can be passed through heavy rollers to curve them or they can be bent by presses.

The steel is joined by welding. In shipbuilding, unlike car manufacture, a very strong watertight joint is needed between the plates, so the edges of the plates are welded solidly together.

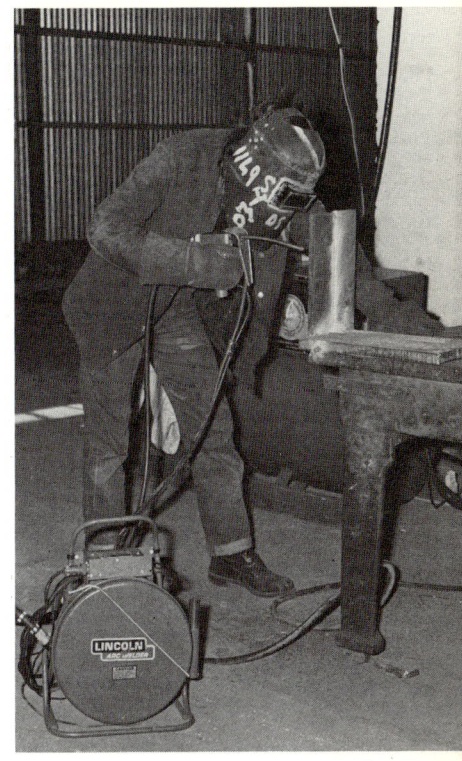

*A welder joining two pieces of steel*

*Cutting steel by remote control*

*Shipyards at Sunderland, showing the covered berths in which the ships are built*

*Assembling a ship under cover*

*Steel being used in the foundations of a new power station*

The shipyard consists of a berth, on which the ship is built, surrounded by large workshops. In the workshops plates and sections are welded together to make sub-assemblies which are then combined to make larger units.

Often work will continue in this way, under cover, until a whole section of the ship, such as the stern, has been completed. Then this big section is moved into the open and put in position on the berth's slipway.

Some shipyards now have covered berths or docks so that ships are built completely under cover in factory conditions and floated out with only the final outfitting to be done.

When the main sections of the ship have been welded together and some of the heaviest equipment, such as the engines and propeller, put in place, the ship is ready to be launched and taken to the fitting-out basin. Here the ship is equipped with steering gear, controls, cargo-handling machinery, electrical and refrigerating plant—everything that is needed to change a floating steel box into an ocean-going ship.

### Civil engineering and construction

Steel is important in building, particularly in large-scale undertakings such as motorways, bridges, tunnels, oil installations, hospitals, shopping centres and tall buildings.

It is used to make a strong framework of steel beams to which other building materials, particularly concrete, can be added. The concrete is further strengthened by steel rods. If you pass a building site you can often see the girders or rods sticking out of partly finished concrete.

*Iron and steel*

When civil engineers need equipment specially made (such as giant turbines for power stations), they work closely with the steel manufacturers. Civil engineers also need earth-moving equipment and cranes, all produced by industries using iron and steel.

## Using other metals and alloys: building aircraft

Iron and steel are not the only metals that industry needs. Copper is the only one widely used in its pure state. The others (aluminium, magnesium, manganese, nickel, zinc, tungsten, titanium) are usually made into *alloys*.

An alloy is a material made from a mixture of metals and it is more useful than a pure metal. Iron and steel are themselves alloys of iron and carbon.

Alloys are an important material in aircraft building. The outer skin and framework of an aircraft must be as light as possible, so aluminium is used. But aluminium is a soft metal, so to make it harder and stronger small amounts of other metals are added. This makes an alloy which is three times as strong as steel.

*Earth-moving machinery*

*Assembling the nose of a small jet passenger plane*

*An aircraft factory. In the foreground the wings are being assembled*

*Iron and steel*

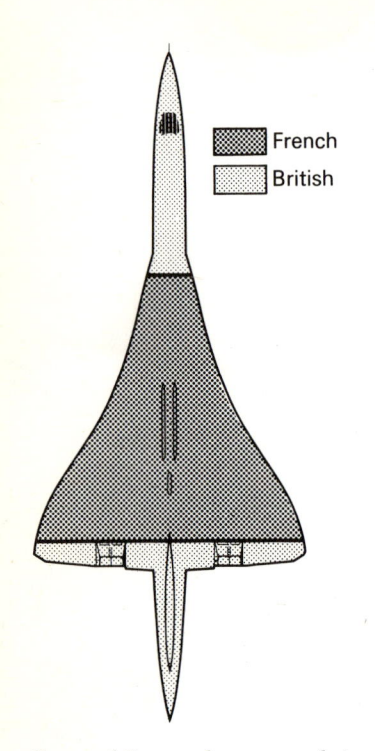

French
British

Machined aluminium alloy
Rolled aluminium alloy
Steel
Resin bonded glass fibre

*The materials used in Concorde*

*Parts of Concorde were made in Britain and parts in France*

*Britain's main aircraft factories*

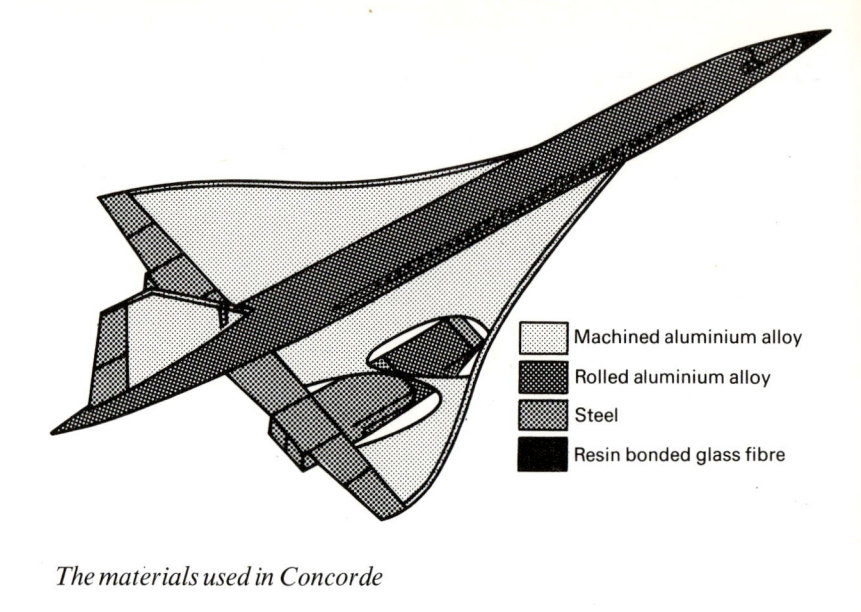

When Concorde is flying it has to withstand very low temperatures (−15 °C) when it is climbing or descending and very high temperatures (up to 153 °C at the tip of its nose) when it is flying at supersonic speeds. So the designers chose a special aluminium alloy for much of the outside skin, high-temperature steel and stainless steel for parts carrying heavy loads and for the front edges of the wings, and a special plastic strengthened with glass fibre for the nose.

Like a ship, an aircraft is built by preparing sub-assemblies which are then made into larger sections. Unlike a ship, however, the sections may be made in different factories, perhaps even in different countries.

Concorde is one example of this. The wings and the central fuselage were built in France. The nose, front fuselage and tail, together with the engines, were made in Britain. Each country supplied the other with parts so that aircraft could be assembled in Britain and in Europe. Another example is the European Airbus: the British aircraft industry makes the wings for this aircraft at Chester.

Britain's main airliner factories are at Hatfield, north of London (the Airbus and a small jet plane), at Filton, Bristol (Concorde) and at Weybridge (Concorde and the BAC One-Eleven airliner). Other factories produce parts for these aircraft and build planes for the Royal Navy and the Royal Air Force.

# Glass

Britain has one of the biggest glass-making industries in the world. St Helens in Merseyside is an important centre for making glass. The industry was set up here because the raw materials were close at hand: sand, limestone and soda ash (made from salt obtained from large deposits in Cheshire). Most importantly, there was coal which, in the past, was used for firing the furnaces.

## Making glass

Sand, limestone, soda ash and broken glass, called *cullet*, are mixed and put in a furnace. They are heated and at temperatures up to 1600 °C they fuse together to make a sticky mass of molten glass.

For large-scale production a tank furnace is used; it can hold up to 2000 tonnes of glass. The tank furnace is in the form of a bath. The raw materials are fed in continuously at one end and molten glass is taken out of the other.

## Flat glass

Much of the glass we see around us is called "flat glass". It is used for windows, shop fronts and for the windscreens of cars and aircraft.

It is made by a process known as the *float*. A ribbon of hot liquid glass up to three metres wide moves out of the furnace and floats

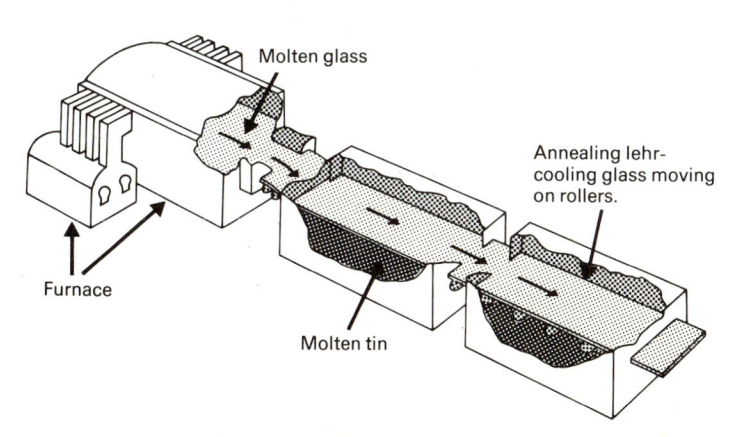

*The cutting-machine control room in a modern float-glass plant*

*Making float glass*

*Moulding milk bottles. Hollow lumps of red-hot glass are moved into a mould where they are blown to their final shape and come out as finished bottles. The diagram below explains what happens*

*Making jars: molten glass is forced into a mould by a plunger (1 and 2). The shaped glass (3) is moved to a jar-shaped mould (4) and blown into its final shape (5) by compressed air to make the finished jar (6)*

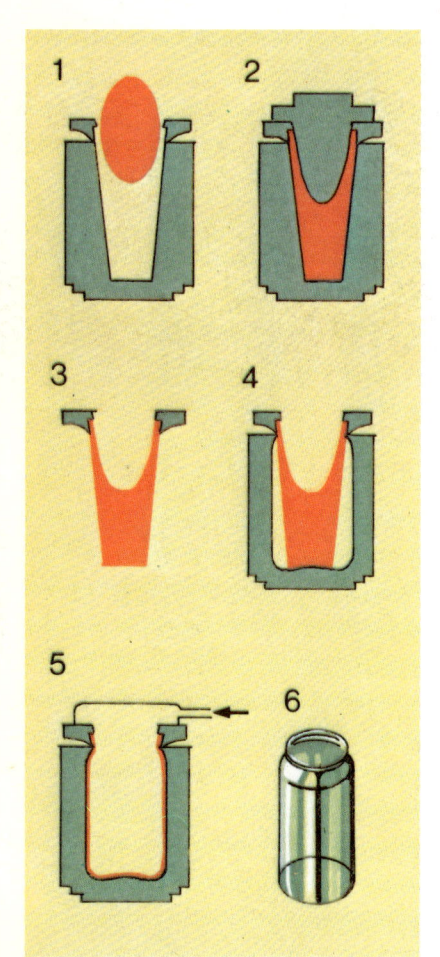

along the surface of a bath of molten tin. The surface of this molten tin is flat, so the ribbon of glass moving across it also becomes flat.

As the glass moves along the bath, it cools until it is hard enough to leave the float bath. It is then moved on by rollers into a tunnel called a *lehr* for further cooling. This process, called *annealing*, strengthens the glass. Then it is cut automatically and stacked.

### Glass containers

One way of shaping glass is to take a blob of molten glass on the end of a hollow pipe and to blow down the pipe to form a glass bubble which can be shaped with hand tools.

The glass-blower can also use a mould to shape the glass, blowing down the pipe and forcing the glass against the sides of the mould. This method has been adapted to make the millions of bottles and jars needed every day. These are made on huge automatic assembly lines.

To make a jam jar, a gob of molten glass drops from the furnace into the first mould on the machine. This forms the neck of the jar. Then a plunger forces the liquid glass into a thick-walled object which only just resembles a jam jar. In the next mould compressed air blows the glass against the walls of the mould which is the exact shape of the finished jar. The jars then move along the production line for annealing by being reheated and gradually cooled.

# Pottery

When clay and other ingredients such as powdered stone, flint or bone are mixed with water, this becomes a soft clay *body* that can easily be shaped. If it is allowed to dry, it keeps the shape it has been given. But, if it becomes wet, it can be turned back into soft clay again. When the dried clay is *fired* in a furnace, some of the minerals fuse to a form which is rock hard and will keep its shape permanently.

Clay is shaped and fired to make a wide range of products—from bricks and the linings for blast furnaces to the nose cones of space rockets. But we use it every day as cups and saucers, so let's have a look at the way pottery is made.

### The clay

Most of the pottery made in Britain comes from an area in Staffordshire called "the Potteries". The industry grew up here over the centuries because there was clay for making earthenware and coal for firing the kilns. Nowadays most of the clay comes from other places. Ball clay, which is added to earthenware to give it strength, comes from Devon or Dorset, and china clay comes from Cornwall.

Different mixtures of clay are used for the different kinds of pottery and there are several clays in each *body*. At the factory the clays are mixed with water. Then hard materials such as bone, flints and feldspars, ground to a fine powder, are added to prevent the pottery from cracking during firing.

### Shaping the pottery

Sometimes the clay is *thrown* on to a revolving wheel and is shaped by the potter who uses his hands to work the material. Jugs and teapots are *cast* by having liquid clay poured into a plaster-of-Paris mould. The plaster soaks up the water, leaving a layer of solid clay inside the mould.

*(Above) Throwing a pot on the wheel. (Below) Taking a cast pot out of its mould*

*Making plates*

*Pushing a truck of pottery into a tunnel kiln for firing*

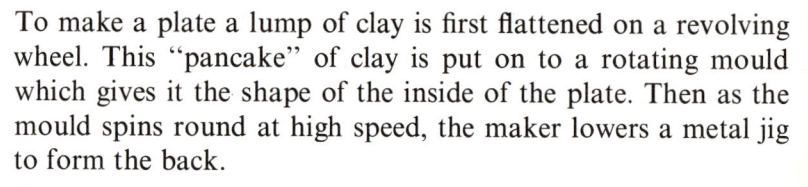

*Filling in transfer outlines by hand*

To make a plate a lump of clay is first flattened on a revolving wheel. This "pancake" of clay is put on to a rotating mould which gives it the shape of the inside of the plate. Then as the mould spins round at high speed, the maker lowers a metal jig to form the back.

### Firing the pottery

When the clay has been shaped it is allowed to dry. Then it is fired in a tunnel kiln. This is heated by gas or by electricity. The pottery is placed on trucks which are moved slowly through the tunnel until they reach the maximum heat. Then they begin to cool until, at the far end of the tunnel, they are cool enough to handle. The firing may take a few hours or more than two days. Often there are several firings.

After the first firing the pottery is dipped in a liquid glaze and is fired again. Now it is smooth, with a sparkling glossy surface. Some of the pieces have patterns printed on them by machines. Others are impressed with colour transfers by hand.

The plastic backing of the transfer burns away in the next firing, leaving the coloured patterns on the china. Transfer outlines of patterns can be filled in by hand with different coloured enamels. Most of the fine bone chinaware also has a line added in gold, platinum or colour.

# Clothing

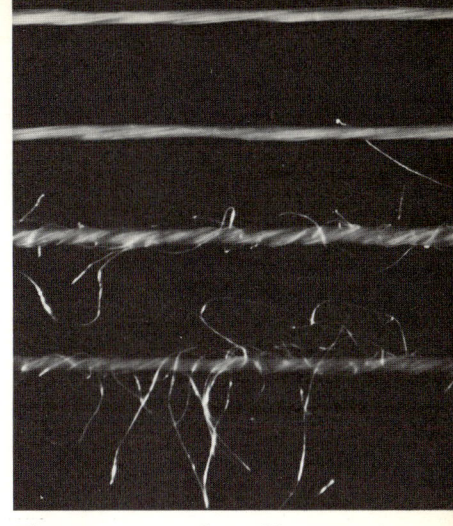

Most clothes are woven or knitted from yarn. The yarn may look rather like knitting wool, if it is intended for making winter-coat material, or like very fine sewing thread, if it is meant for a lightweight fabric.

Some of the yarn is made from natural fibres such as wool or cotton, some from man-made fibres such as polyester or nylon. Some is made from a mixture of both.

The fibres come in two forms, filament and staple.

## Filament fibres

A filament is a long unbroken thread. The only natural fibre that is used as a filament is silk. This is obtained by unwinding the silk from the cocoon of the silk moth. The filament is so fine that the threads from seven cocoons are put together to make a yarn that is heavy enough to be woven.

Silk has always been expensive to produce. For this reason silk was the first fibre that scientists tried to imitate. The first successful "artificial silk" was *viscose rayon*. Chemists working on ways of making paper from wood pulp produced a golden-yellow syrupy substance. When this was forced through fine holes, a filament was made which could be used in much the same way as a filament of real silk.

Most man-made fibres (see pages 15–17) are made into a filament. Sometimes the filament is used to make a fine delicate thread or grouped with other threads to make a thicker yarn which can be knitted or woven. One way of using man-made fibres is to crimp or put a wave into the filament to make it bulkier, and then to cut it into short lengths and to treat it as a staple fibre.

## Staple fibres

Natural fibres such as wool, cotton and linen are staple fibres. The length of the fibres ranges from half a centimetre for some cottons to fifty centimetres for linen.

*The top two strands are filaments of viscose rayon. Those below have been cut into staple fibre and spun into thread*

*Some of the jets used in making rayon fibres*

*The viscose is forced through jets in a bath of acid. All the filaments from one jet, thousands at a time, form one of the threads you can see*

## Clothing

### Wool

This is one of the oldest natural fibres used for making yarn. Some wool is produced in Britain (see page 61) but most of the wool used in the woollen industries of West Yorkshire, Scotland and the West Country, comes from Australia and New Zealand. The British woollen industry is the largest in the world and exports the cloth it produces to countries throughout the world.

### Cotton

This vegetable fibre is grown in sub-tropical countries. It has been imported into Britain for many centuries. For a long time mills in Lancashire spun the cotton into yarn and made cloth which was then exported, often to the countries which had grown the cotton. Now these countries have their own cotton mills and the demand for British-made cotton has grown less. Some cotton mills have been closed and others have been reorganized so that they spin and weave a wide variety of man-made fibres as well as cotton.

## Making yarn

Have you ever tried twisting a thread from a tuft of sheep's wool found on a hedge? If you have, you know that part twists easily but that other parts form a lump or break.

Before fibres are spun into a yarn, they have to be prepared. The finished yarn needs to be even in thickness all along its length and the fibres in it must lie along the yarn to make it strong and hold it together. All the machines in the spinning mill are designed to turn a higgledy-piggledy mass of fibres into a strong even yarn. They do this by stages, and all the time the strand of fibre is being produced, it becomes longer, finer and stronger.

*Sorting wool into different qualities*

*Washing wool to remove dirt and grease. Here it is coming out of the final rinse*

Natural fibres are usually dirty. The dry dirt and bits of stalk and leaf in raw cotton can be removed by beating and shaking the fibres and blowing them through pipes. Wool is sorted into grades of fineness and then it is washed several times in hot soapy water and then dried.

*Carding*

If you lay your piece of wool on a brush and stroke another brush over it, always working in the same direction, you will find that the fibres begin to lie smoothly side by side. If you try to make a thread now, you find that you can pull them out into a much thinner strand. This twists into a thread more easily.

In the spinning mill this job is done by a carding machine. A soft mass of fibre goes in at one end, passes between rollers covered in wire spikes and comes out at the other end as a soft loose rope of fibre called a *sliver*. This is coiled into a big metal can.

If a very smooth fabric is being made, a sliver of wool or cotton of a long-staple type is passed through a combing machine. This removes all the short fibres and makes a new sliver of long fibres which can be spun into a very smooth yarn.

*Carding machines produce a soft rope of fibre called a "sliver"*

*When the sliver has been drawn out into a thinner rope, it is coiled into cans*

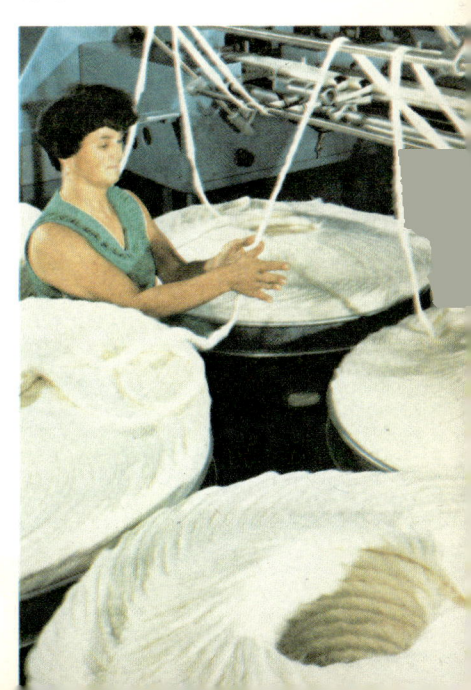

*Drawing and twisting the loose sliver into a "roving" which is wound on bobbins*

## Spinning

The sliver is too thick to spin so it has to be drawn out into a much thinner rope, with a slight twist to prevent it from breaking when it is spun. This lightly twisted strand is called a *roving*. It is strong enough to be wound on to bobbins which fit on to the spinning machine.

The spinning machine draws the strand out still further and twists it into a yarn which is wound on to cardboard tubes to make a "package of yarn". Some are cone-shaped. The ones with straight sides are called *cheeses* because they look like big uncut cheeses.

If yarn is to be dyed before it is made into cloth, it is wound into skeins so that the dye can reach every strand.

*Spinning the roving into fine yarn*

*"Cheeses" of yarn*

*A large cotton-weaving shed*

*Knitting jumpers*

## Making cloth

### Weaving

In simple weaving a crosswise thread (the *weft* thread) passes under and over the lengthwise threads (the *warp* threads) on a weaving machine called a loom. The loom separates the warp threads so that some are raised above the others. Then a shuttle carrying the weft passes through this gap, over some warp threads and under others. In some modern looms there is no shuttle and the weft thread is carried across the warp threads by a jet of water or air.

Different kinds of cloth can be made by varying the way in which the threads cross (under one, over two and so on).

### Knitting

Many fabrics are produced by knitting rather than weaving. Wool, acrylic, cotton, nylon and polyester jersey are knitted for suits, trousers, shirts and blouses. To see whether a material has been knitted or woven you have to look very closely at it.

### Dyeing and finishing

Most cloth is dyed after it has been woven. Cotton and linen are bleached first and then they are either dyed or printed with a pattern. Woollen cloth is dyed. Its surface may be brushed to produce a fluffy look or, if a smooth suiting is wanted, a worsted cloth is passed through a machine rather like a lawnmower which cuts cuts off any long hairs or fluff.

Finally the cloth is pressed and made into rolls which are sent to the clothing factories.

*Checking woven cloth for flaws*

*Placing the pattern on the cloth*

*Cutting through many layers of cloth at once*

*Pressing the finished coat*

**Making a coat**

Most of our clothes are made in factories. What happens when a winter coat is made?

The cloth chosen for the coat is unrolled and spread out on a long table. More layers of cloth are spread on top until there are about fifty to a hundred thicknesses in all. The pattern for the coat is laid out on the cloth with great care. The warp threads in the cloth, the *grain*, must run straight up and down the coat to allow it to hang properly. When two pieces of the coat are stitched together, checks and patterns must match up.

A special cutting machine called a straight-knife cuts the layers of cloth into smaller pieces and then a bandknife is used to cut exactly round each pattern piece.

A tailor marks each piece of cut-out cloth with chalk to show the machinist where to place a pocket or some other detail. Then teams of men and women stitch the coats together, each one working on one part, a pocket perhaps or a sleeve.

The workroom has very fast sewing machines and special machines to make buttonholes, oversew the cut edges of fabric and stitch hems invisibly.

When the coat has been stitched together, it is checked to see that it has been made properly and that it is the correct size. It is carefully pressed in a steam press. Then the lining is stitched in and the buttons sewn on. Finally the coat is checked again and then it is ready to be packed and sent to the shops.

# Maps, scales and contours

Peter and Oliver are brothers and they share a bedroom. Jenny is their sister, with her own bedroom. Here are the plans they drew of their rooms. You'll see that Jenny's drawing is larger than Peter and Oliver's. Does this mean that her room is larger? Is there anything in the drawings which gives a clue about the size of the rooms?

You can find a clue in the sizes of the beds in the two rooms. A single bed is nearly 2 metres long and just under 1 metre wide. It looks as though Jenny's drawing is drawn on a much larger scale than Peter and Oliver's. If you measure one of the beds in the boys' room you will find that they have drawn a 2-metre bed as a rectangle 2 centimetres long. This means they have used a scale of 1 centimetre to 1 metre (100 centimetres). We can write this as 1:100. This is a scale that architects and builders use. What scale has Jenny used?

Because Jenny was drawing a small room, she could use a large scale. If you are making a plan of something large, you need to use a different scale to suit the subject.

*A corner of Peter and Oliver's room*

*Jenny's room*

Here is a photograph of the castle at Richmond in North Yorkshire. You can see the keep and the big open space, shaped like a triangle, within the castle walls. Behind the castle lies the big market place of Richmond

Here is a plan of the castle, drawn to a scale of 1:1250, the largest scale used by the Ordnance Survey, the government department which makes maps. On this plan 1 centimetre represents 12·5 metres

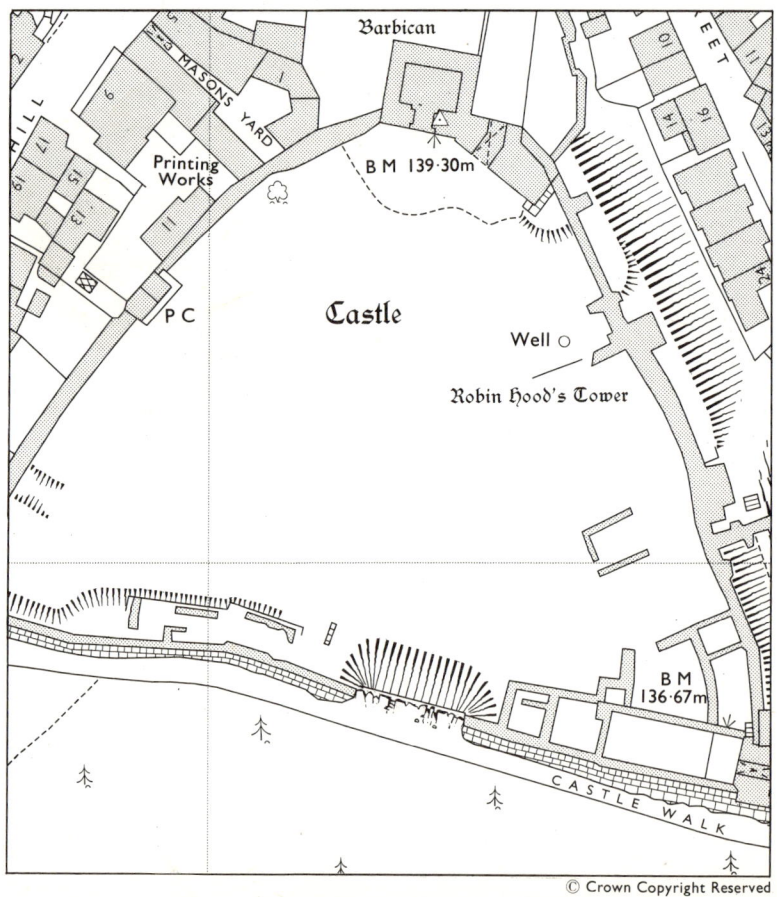

C42

*Maps, scales and contours*

If you look at the map on page 42, you can see that the castle takes up nearly all the space. In the photograph you can see not only the castle but also the market place and the church which stands in the middle of it. It would take a whole page of this book to show all this at the scale of 1:1250. But on a 1:2500-scale map the castle and market place can be shown in half a page. This smaller-scale map shows the same details as the larger-scale one but it is half the size. One centimetre represents 25 metres.

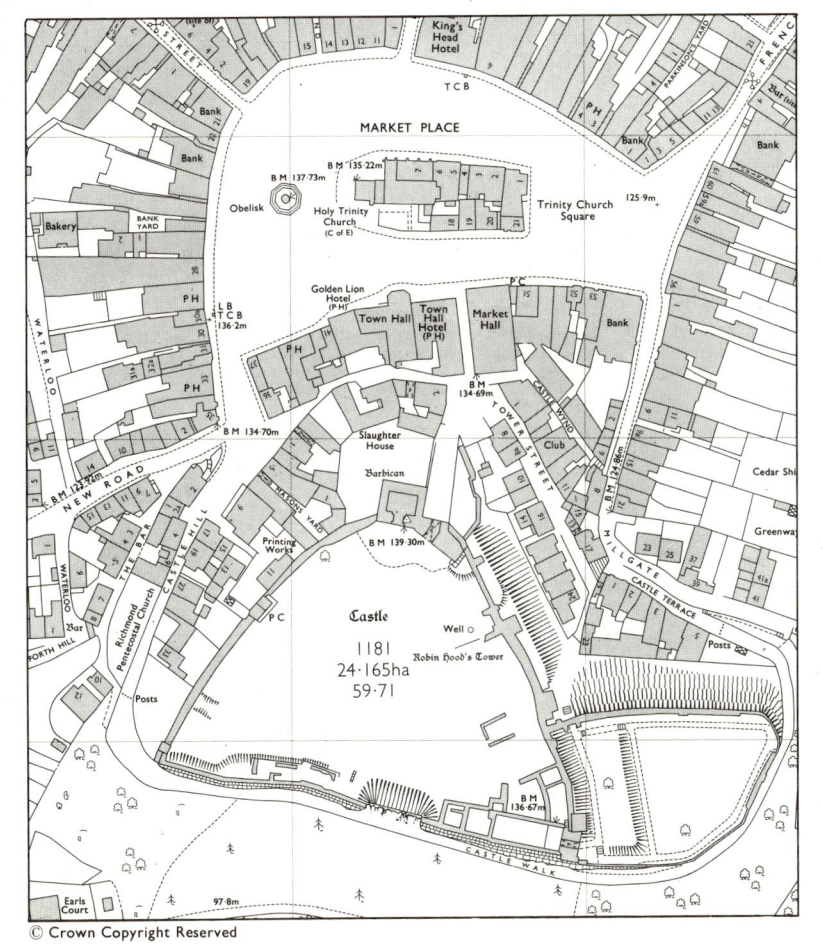

*This map is drawn to a smaller scale, 1:2500*

*One centimetre represents 25 metres*

*Here is the market place photographed from a different direction. Can you find the church and the obelisk on the map?*

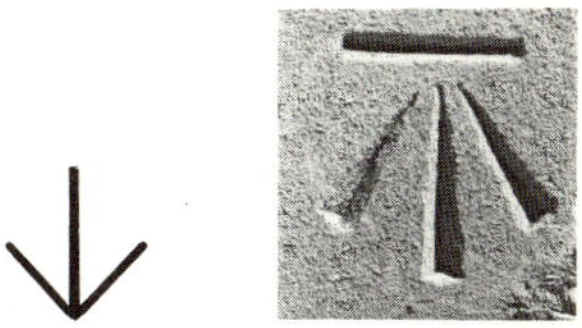

*(Left) How a bench mark is drawn on a map (Right) How a bench mark looks on a wall*

## Showing height on maps

If you look carefully at these maps, you see that in some places the height above sea-level is given, for instance, "B M 139.30m" (B M means "bench mark", a term used by mapmakers for the exact spot used for measuring height above sea-level).

Can you find a bench mark near your home? Your school or library will have a 1:1250 or 1:2500 map of your district. Find out where the bench marks are on the map and see if you can find them in the streets near your home.

*On a large-scale map a steep slope is shown by these lines. The thicker end of the line shows the higher part of the slope*

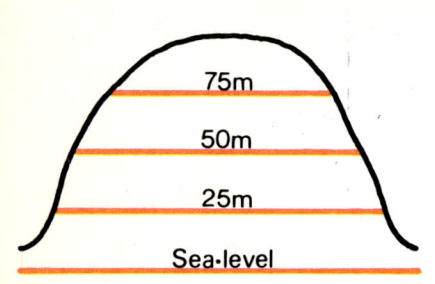

*A slice through a hill, showing the contour lines*

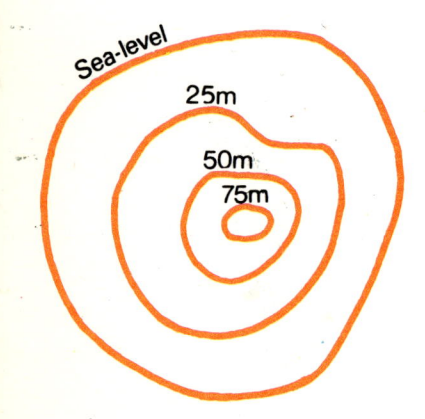

*This is how contour lines appear on a map*

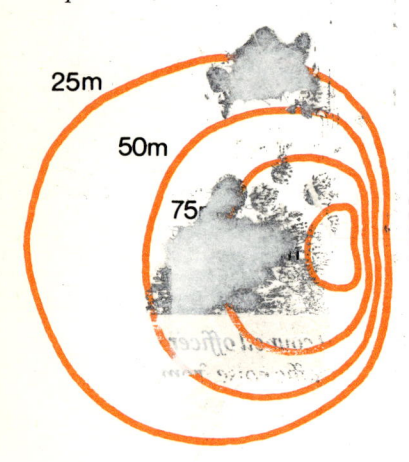

*Look at this map of a hill. What can you tell about the shape of the hill from the contour lines?*

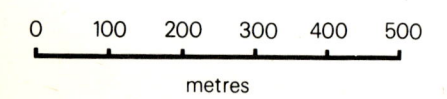

## Maps, scales and contours

The map below is drawn at a scale of 1:10 000 (1 centimetre represents 100 metres). At this scale, or at smaller scales still, there is no room to put in details of heights and bench marks. Instead, the mapmakers draw in *contour lines*, lines which join together all the places which are a certain height above sea-level.

Imagine a hill in very flat country. One day there is a flood and the water rises to a height of 5 metres above sea-level. The line the water makes round the sides of the hill is a contour line because everything along it is 5 metres above sea-level.

If the water rises another 5 metres, another contour line is made by the water: this is the 10-metre contour line.

The map on this page has contour lines drawn on it in red. The difference in height between one line and the next is 5 metres. Sometimes the contour lines are far apart on the map. This means that the land slopes gently. Sometimes they are close together (look along the river banks by Richmond Castle). This means that the land is very steep.

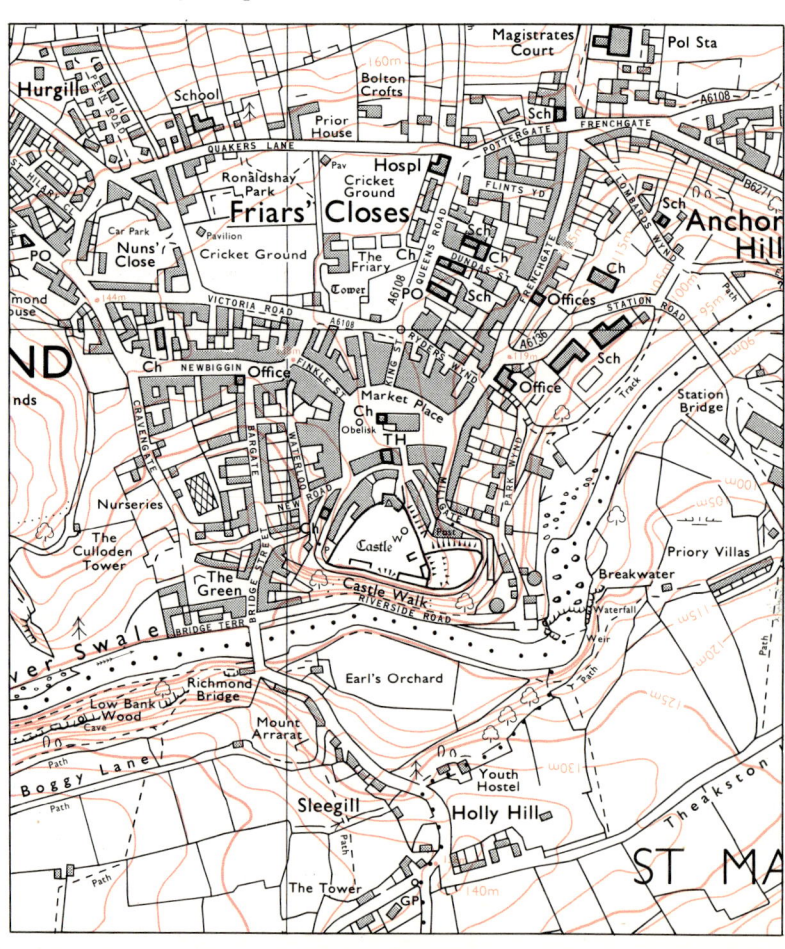

44

# A town and its services

Every day we want our homes to be supplied with pure water, gas and electricity. We expect our dustbins to be emptied and the streets round our homes to be cleaned regularly and to be well lit at night. If we are in trouble, we want to be able to dial "999" for the police, an ambulance or the fire service. We need doctors and hospitals, teachers and schools, libraries, museums, sports halls and swimming pools.

Some of these things are provided by the local or *district council*. Others are provided by the much bigger *county council* in England and Wales or by the *regional council* in Scotland.

## The district council

The men and women who form the district council are elected by the people who live in the district. The district council's work includes building houses for rent, collecting refuse and making sure that the food sold in shops or served in restaurants is safe to eat. It also provides parks, theatres and other places where people can relax and enjoy themselves.

The district council shares some work with the much bigger county council. Between them they organize social services for people who need help (the old and disabled, for instance). They decide how land should be used (for industry, farming, homes, offices or shops), what new roads should be built and what buildings should be put up.

*Servicing street lights*

*A district council ... level of traffic noise from ...*

*Looking after the local park*

*The library service is organized by the county council*

*A town and its services*

## County council

The county council is also elected. It organizes services for the county as a whole. It provides schools and colleges of further education, libraries and museums. It is responsible for the police and the fire brigade, two of the emergency services we can call on.

Where does the money for all these services come from? It comes from rates, a tax charged on the value of buildings, and from the government. Ask your parents to show you the note which comes with the demand for the rates. It tells you how the district and county councils spend the money they raise in rates.

## Other services

The district and county councils don't provide all the services we need. For instance, health services (hospitals, health centres, clinics and ambulance services) are provided by the area health authority. It also organizes the family-doctor service.

Some government departments have local offices. For instance, in most towns the Department of Employment has job centres and the Department of the Environment has driving-test centres.

Let's look at two very important services, one provided by the district and county councils and one by a big area authority.

*Hospitals are run by health authorities*

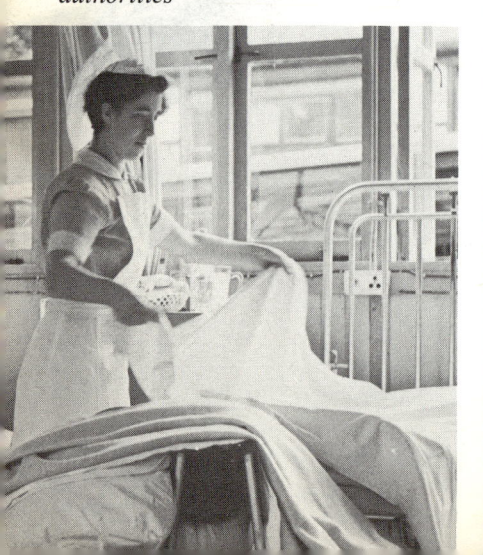

*The police service and the fire brigade are also county services*

*Collecting refuse from homes*

*Keeping the streets clean*

# Refuse

Every household fills its dustbin with rubbish of all kinds: paper, plastic, packages, waste food and junk. Factories, offices, hospitals, schools and shops produce even more. The district council collects the rubbish. Much of it is lightweight plastic and paper. The refuse vehicle compresses the refuse as it collects it so that a heavier load can be carried. Clean waste paper and cardboard are salvaged and sold to paper mills.

*Tipping rubbish on waste land*

Most of the refuse collected is tipped on to waste land—low-lying or uneven ground. The rubbish is covered with layers of earth so that paper does not blow away. When the tip has been left for several years to settle down, the ground can be used for agriculture or for playing fields. The rest of the rubbish is burned in large incinerators.

When a site is chosen as a rubbish tip, the council makes sure that the rubbish will not pollute water supplies or harm the environment. ("Environment" means "surroundings" but, when we use this word, we are talking about the quality of the surroundings in which we live. Is the air polluted, are there trees and gardens, are the streams and rivers clean, are the streets clogged with traffic?)

## A town and its services

# Water

We take water for granted—until there is a drought or a river overflows. The water which comes through our taps is supplied by a water authority, a big regional body which provides water for several counties.

You know that the water which comes from the tap once fell as rain, flowing down the hillsides in streams or sinking down through the rock until it forms underground streams and lakes. Sometimes these streams bubble to the surface and form springs. Sometimes wells are sunk to reach underground water.

The water authority draws water supplies from streams, rivers, springs and wells. Often local supplies are not sufficient for big cities such as those of the Midlands. These cities may use mountain water. This is rain which falls on the mountains, in Wales perhaps, and is collected in reservoirs, built by putting dams across river valleys. The water is carried to the cities by pipes which are laid so that the water can flow downhill all the way.

In other parts of the country water is stored in reservoirs, so that there is a good supply of water for times when the rainfall is low. Reservoirs are often used for sailing and fishing.

Before water can be used, it must be purified. First it passes through a bed of coarse sand. This removes much of the dirt. Then the water is passed through a bed of fine sand which takes out any remaining dirt and also some of the bacteria which live in water. Finally the water flows into a covered tank where it is treated with chlorine to kill any remaining germs.

*Sailing on a reservoir*

*Water moves in a cycle. It falls as rain on the hills and is cleaned for our use. When we have made it dirty, it is cleaned again and put back in the rivers and the sea. There it evaporates and forms rain clouds*

*Filter beds for cleaning water. You can see some newly prepared beds of clean sand*

*A water tower*

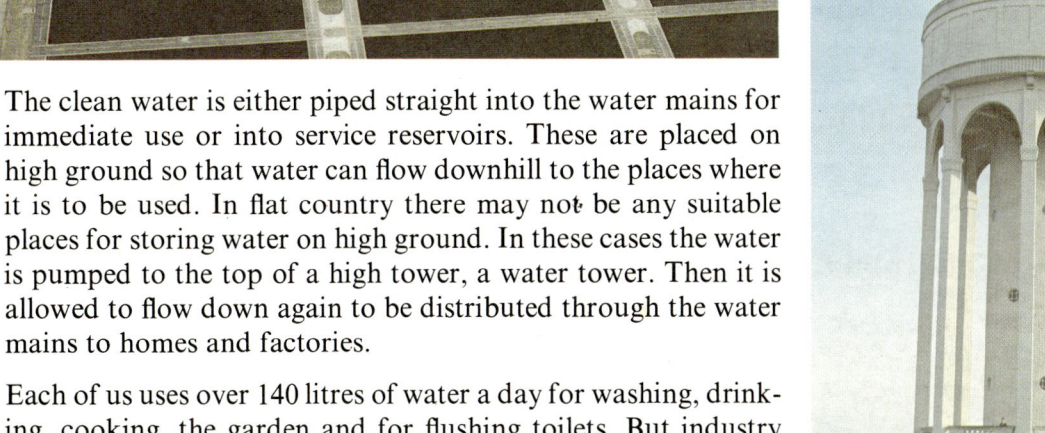

The clean water is either piped straight into the water mains for immediate use or into service reservoirs. These are placed on high ground so that water can flow downhill to the places where it is to be used. In flat country there may not be any suitable places for storing water on high ground. In these cases the water is pumped to the top of a high tower, a water tower. Then it is allowed to flow down again to be distributed through the water mains to homes and factories.

Each of us uses over 140 litres of water a day for washing, drinking, cooking, the garden and for flushing toilets. But industry uses huge quantities of water. Nearly 200 000 litres are needed in the manufacture of one tonne of steel and over 400 000 litres in the making of a car.

*Rivers* The water authorities are also responsible for looking after rivers. Many rivers are polluted with chemicals from factories and farms and with slurry (liquid manure). A river can take in a good deal of waste and, through the action of useful bacteria in the water, can make the waste harmless. But, if there is too much waste, the river loses the oxygen from its water and without oxygen the useful bacteria cannot do their work. Instead, harmful bacteria (which can survive without oxygen) take over. Fish and plant life die and the river becomes an evil-smelling sewer.

*A scientist checks river water for pollution by examining the fish that live in it*

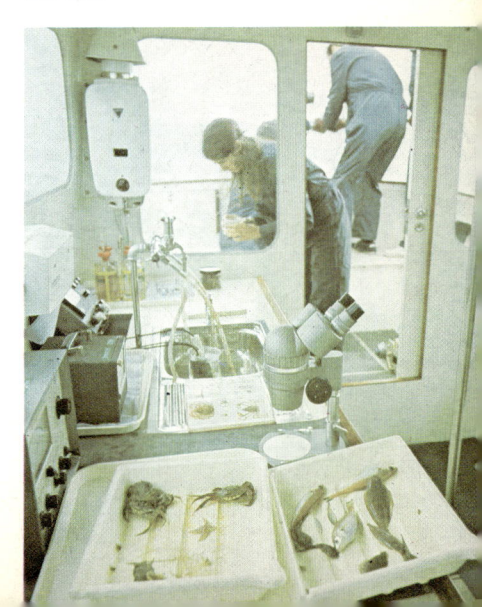

The water authority has the duty of cleaning the rivers. One way is to encourage big industrial plants, which use huge quantities of water, to purify the water before it is released into the rivers. In the lower reaches of the Thames there are paper mills, sugar refineries, distilleries, soap and detergent factories, oil refineries and other plants which use water. Gradually they are changing their processes and installing new equipment so that dirty water does not flow into the Thames.

## A town and its services

*Sewage* An essential part of the water authority's work is the removal and treatment of sewage.

Waste water from houses, factories, shops and offices flows along underground pipes called sewers. In some places rainwater passes through street drains into the sewers too but in others it has a separate system which takes it straight to streams and rivers. Sewers run downhill: small sewers flow into larger ones. The largest sewers are big underground tunnels.

The dirty waste water is taken by the sewerage system to a sewage works where bacteria are used to purify the water and to break down harmful substances (imitating what happens in a healthy river).

First the water in the sewage is separated from the solids. The water needs oxygen so it is sprayed on to clinker beds or compressed air is passed into it. The oxygen enables useful bacteria to purify the water until it is safe to go into a river.

The solid matter from the sewage, the crude sludge, is pumped into tanks where bacteria can work on the waste. The harmful materials are turned by the bacteria into sludge gas which contains methane (see page 9). This gas is used to produce electricity for use within the sewage works. The sludge that is left is harmless and can be used as a fertilizer or it can be taken out to sea where it provides food for tiny sea plants. These are eaten in turn by small sea creatures and then these are eaten by bigger fish.

*Inside a sewer*

*A sewage treatment plant*

# Day, night and the seasons

**The sun gives light and warmth to the earth**

The sun is a gigantic mass of flaming gases more than a million times the size of the earth. The heat of the sun would scorch up anything near it. But the earth is 150 million kilometres from the sun—far enough away not to be scorched to a cinder, yet near enough to receive the light and warmth which make life possible. Without the sun the earth would be so cold that no living thing could survive, and there would be complete darkness.

The earth spins round once in every twenty-four hours. The sun can light only the side of the earth which faces it, so the rest of the earth, away from the sun, is in darkness. During twenty-four hours each part of the earth has one day and one night. When there is daylight in Britain there is darkness in the Pacific Ocean. When there is darkness in Britain there is daylight in the Pacific.

*When there is daylight in Britain (B) there is darkness on the Pacific Ocean (P)*

**The earth goes round the sun**

As well as spinning on its own axis, the earth makes a long journey round the sun. The time taken by the earth to travel once round the sun is one *year*.

*The earth's journey round the sun. The earth is always tilted and this brings different parts of the earth closer to the sun at different seasons of the year*

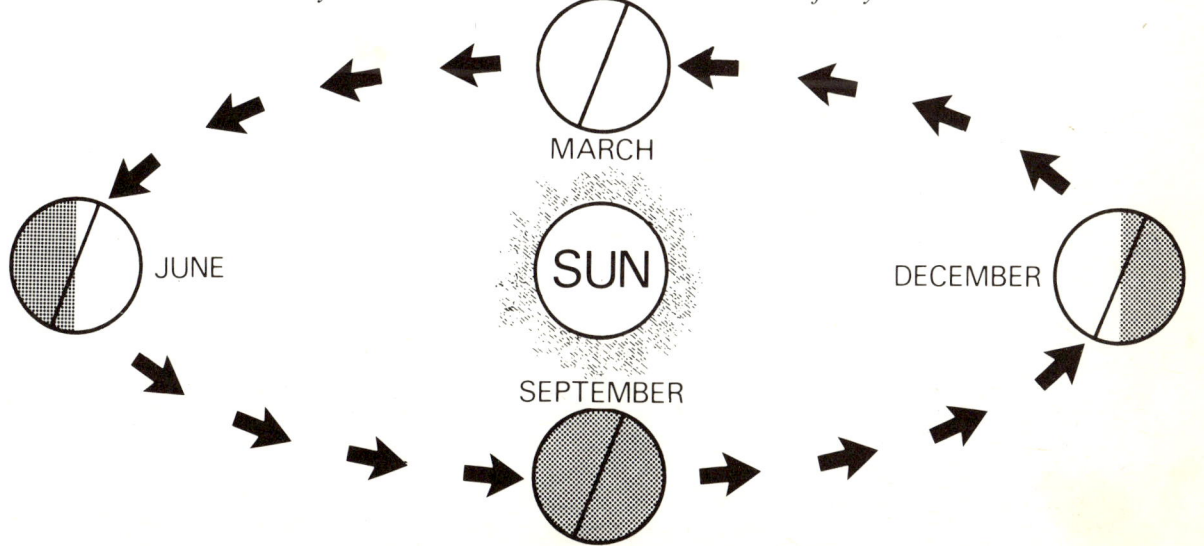

*Day, night and the seasons*

### The earth is tilted as it spins

If a torch shines straight on to a book in a darkened room the page is brightly lit. But if the torch shines at a low angle the page is dimly lit, because the same amount of light is spread over more of the page. In the same way the sun's rays may strike the earth directly from overhead or at a low angle.

The sun gives most heat when it is directly overhead, so countries at the Equator are hotter than countries nearer the Poles. But as the earth travels round the sun it is not spinning upright but is tilted.

From March to September the northern hemisphere (or half) is tilted towards the sun. Then the sun is overhead in countries a little to the north of the Equator and Britain has its summer. The southern hemisphere is tilted away from the sun so Australia has winter.

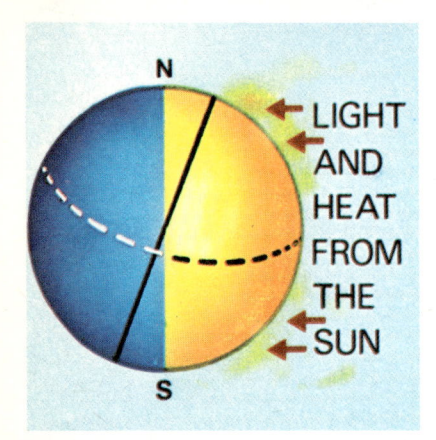

From September to March the southern hemisphere is tilted towards the sun. Then it is summer in Australia and winter in Britain. Christmas Day in Britain is usually cold. But some Australians have their Christmas dinner on the beach, sitting in the sunshine.

If one travels northwards from the Equator in June, the further north one goes the longer are the days. This is because the earth is tilted. At the North Pole in summer there is no darkness, even at night. Even in the north of Scotland the June sky is never really dark. But at all times of the year the hours of darkness and daylight together add up to twenty-four hours.

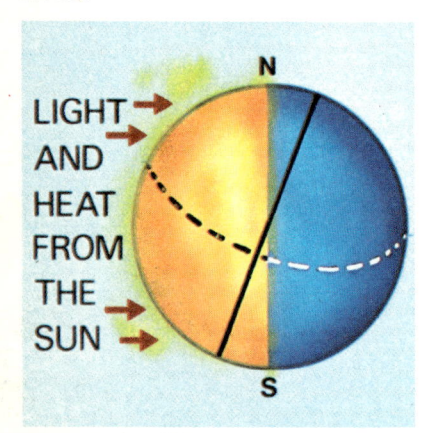

### The sun in summer and winter

In summer the sun rises in the north-east and sinks in the north-west. At midday it is high in the sky and casts short shadows. On a sunny day in the middle of winter the sun is never very high in the sky, and so it casts long shadows. In winter the sun rises in the south-east and sets in the south-west.

*From March to September the northern hemisphere is tilted towards the sun*

*From September to March the southern hemisphere is tilted towards the sun*

# Britain's weather

On the Canadian Prairie in the middle of winter it is bitterly cold. Anyone going out-of-doors wears fur-lined boots and a fur hat, as well as gloves and plenty of warm clothing. But in the summer it is so hot in the Prairie cities that everyone likes to leave the city to travel to the lakes and forests.

Although Britain is about the same distance from the Equator as this part of Canada, its weather is never quite so hot or so cold. Why is this? It is because Britain is surrounded by sea which gets warm slowly and loses its heat slowly. As a result the winds which blow from the sea are never very hot or very cold.

Nor does Britain have a definite wet or dry season, as do the countries of Southern Europe (which have nearly all their rain in winter, and long dry summers). Britain's mild climate, with rain at all times of the year, is called *maritime* (affected by the sea).

*A satellite picture of Britain: the patterns in the clouds are caused by winds over the Scottish mountains*

*A BBC weather map showing an area of high pressure in the Atlantic and north-west winds blowing on Britain*

## Britain's weather

*How a warm wind from the sea brings rain to the hills near the coast*

*Highland and lowland in Britain*

*Winds and rainfall in Britain*

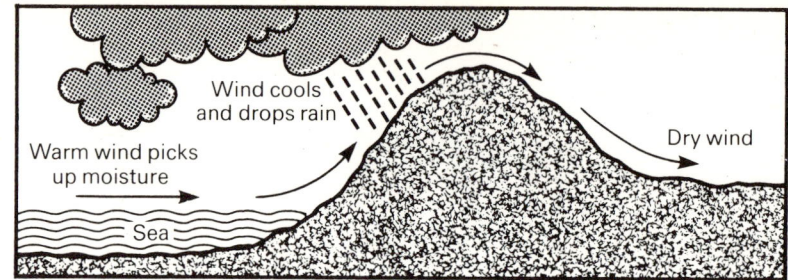

In winter the west of Britain has milder, damper weather than the rest of the country.

The wind which blows most often over Britain is a south-west wind. It is a warm wind in winter because it has blown from warm seas near the Equator, bringing with it a warm sea current called the Gulf Stream. This current warms the seas round Britain.

After a shower on a hot summer's day the warm air dries a wet road very quickly. The water on the road becomes water vapour which is carried by the air. In the same way the south-west wind, blowing over warm seas, picks up moisture.

When the air cools, the water vapour turns back into drops of water. (On a cold day notice how water vapour from a hot bath turns into drops of water again when it meets the cold window pane.)

When the south-west wind reaches Britain it is forced to rise over the land. As it rises it cools, so bringing rain or drizzle to the west of Britain.

Look at the map and notice that most rain falls in the west and that least rain falls in the east.

Rainfall is measured in a rain gauge which shows how much rain has fallen in a certain time. Parts of the Lake District, north-west Scotland and Wales have between 3800 and 5000 millimetres of rain in a year. Parts of south-east England have less than 500 millimetres in a year.

In winter, eastern Britain has drier and colder weather than the rest of Britain

East winds blowing from central Europe are very cold winds, for they come from lands which are far from the sea and which have very cold winters. The cold east winds are dry too, for they have blown over land, not over sea.

In January the Scilly Isles usually have a temperature of 8 °C, while eastern England has less than 4 °C.

54

## Britain's weather

In summer the south of England is warmer than the north of Scotland, because the sun is more nearly overhead in the south. In July the south-west of England has a temperature of 17 °C, while in the north of Scotland it is 13 °C. Farmers in Devon, Cornwall and the Scilly Isles grow early fruit and vegetables and sell them in cooler parts of Britain where the crops ripen later.

Many people go south for their holidays. In summer the south coast is usually the warmest part of Britain. East winds are warm winds in summer, because they are blowing from countries which have hot summer weather.

Although in Britain the weather is usually warm in summer and cool in winter, we cannot forecast the weather for many days in advance. The long-range weather forecasts on radio and television cannot be as accurate as the forecasts for the next day. One day it may be windy, the next day hot and the next rainy. This is because over Britain warm air from the Equator meets cold polar air. Together these two currents of air cause unsettled weather. The warm wet air is forced to rise over the cold air and, as it does so, the water vapour in the air turns to rain. The barometer "falls" and we know that there is a depression over Britain. Then winds are often strong and there may be storms.

Sometimes in summer the area of depressions moves north, over Iceland and Norway. Then Britain has long periods of fine weather, with clear skies and very little wind. The barometer "rises" and we may even have a heat wave. We say that there is an *anticyclone* over Britain.

During an anticyclone in winter it is usually cold and frosty at night, with clear skies. In November an anticyclone may bring mist and fog.

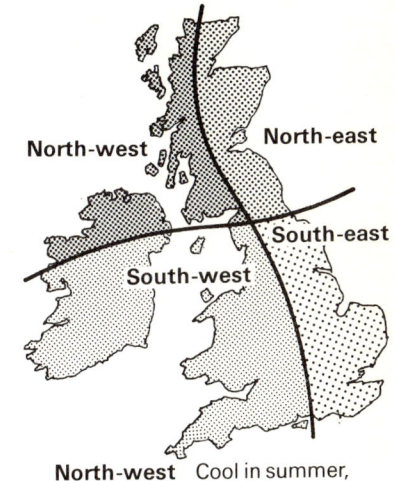

**North-west** Cool in summer, mild in winter
**North-east** Cool in summer, cold in winter
**South-west** Warm in summer, mild in winter
**South-east** Warm in summer, cold in winter

*Britain's weather*

*A weather satellite collects information from stations on the earth's surface and photographs the earth. It also distributes weather reports (WEFAX) which the central station has put together from the satellite's photographs and other information*

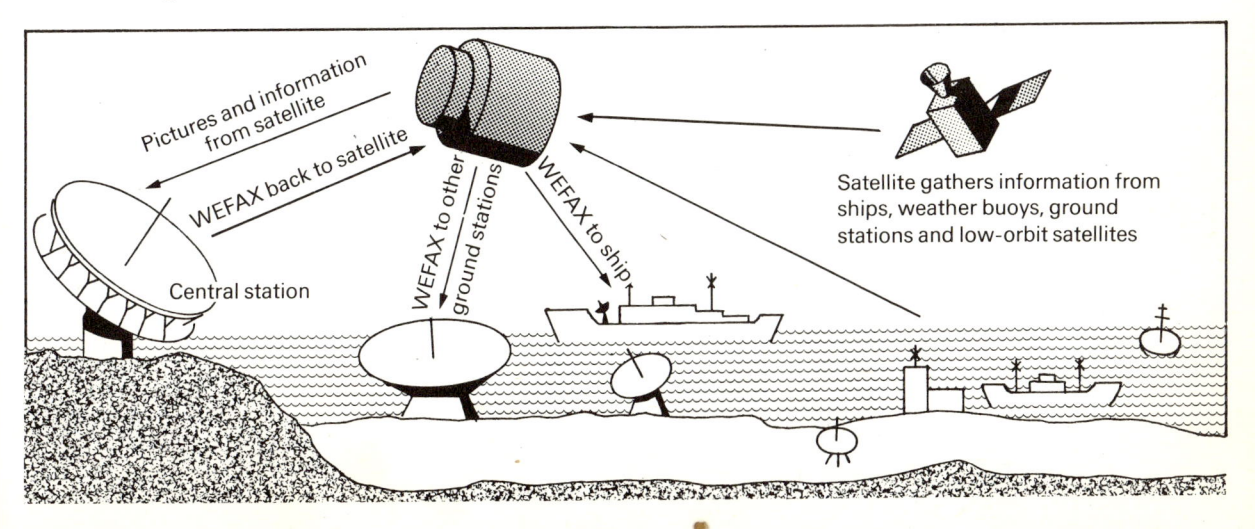

Satellite gathers information from ships, weather buoys, ground stations and low-orbit satellites

# Farming

*Modern farms use powerful machinery to do the work*

*Many farms look like this—an old farmhouse surrounded by modern farm buildings for livestock, machinery and storage*

Although Britain is a crowded country where most people live and work in towns, farming is still one of our most important industries. Our farms produce more than half the food we eat. Fewer than three in every hundred workers actually work in farming; but many more work in industries which are closely related to farming—making agricultural machinery, fertilizers, agricultural chemicals and animal feeding stuffs. Others work with the food from the farms and prepare it for sale: baking bread, cakes, biscuits and pastry, making sweets, preparing meat products, freezing fruit and vegetables and brewing beer and other drinks.

Work on farms follows a different pattern from that in most factories and requires different kinds of skill and knowledge. The farmer has important decisions to make. He has to decide what are the best crops to grow or animals to keep on his particular farm. This depends on the kind of soil he has, how much rain falls, whether the land is hilly or flat and what products will sell best.

He has to take decisions all through the year about the best time for sowing seeds, for harvesting and for cutting grass for winter feed. If he is selling animals, he has to decide whether it is better to keep them a little longer in the hope of a higher price or to sell them at once to save on feeding costs.

*Farming*

## A dairy farm in the West Country

Mr Gray has a farm on the plain of Somerset. It is mainly a dairy farm but he also has a flock of sheep and orchards of cider apples. The farm lies about 30 metres above sea-level and occupies about 112 hectares. The gently sloping fields are divided by hedges.

Enough rain falls during the year to keep the rich clay soil moist so that the grass grows well. The rain also fills the streams and ponds. This is important because animals, particularly milking cows, must have plenty to drink.

Mr Gray keeps about a hundred Friesian cows divided into two herds. This means his stockmen can know each cow and care for it individually. Each cow has a name and, because his Friesian cattle were originally bred in Holland, some of them have Dutch names such as Romkje and Meibloem.

## Grass

Any farmer who keeps cows must grow crops to feed them. Grass is their main food and this is a crop which must be very carefully managed. There must be fresh grazing during the spring, summer and early autumn. There must also be enough to cut and store for use in the winter when no fresh grass grows.

Mr Gray ploughs his fields regularly and reseeds them. To make the most of his grass he uses an electric fence so that the cows feed on one strip of grass at a time. If the cows touch the fence it gives them a slight electric shock.

*Friesian cows are popular with dairy farmers*

*An electric fence keeps the cows to one strip of grass at a time*

*Cutting grass with a forage harvester which blows the grass into the trailer*

*Packing grass into a silage barn*

*Each cow has her own cubicle*

During the early summer the farmer regularly cuts his green grass with a machine called a forage-harvester. Then he packs the grass down in layers in silo barns. Tractors are driven over the grass to press it down. Usually it is treated with a preservative. It is then known as *silage* which is a kind of pickled grass. By the time it is used in the winter it will be a yellow-brown, golden colour and have a strong, slightly vinegary smell.

Later in the summer grass is cut for hay which is dried, baled and stored for winter feeding.

**Looking after the cows**

From April to the end of November the cows are out in the fields day and night. At the beginning of December (earlier in a wet autumn, later when the ground is dry and the grass is still growing) the cows are taken in for the winter.

Each herd has its own cubicle house. These are light airy buildings, designed so that they can be cleaned easily every day. Each cow has her own cubicle or pen. She can move freely from the cubicle house into the yard to the silage barn where she can munch away at the solid mass of silage. During the winter the cows eat their way through this enormous stack of silage, about 6 metres high. An electric fence is used to keep them from trampling the silage and tunnelling their way into it. The stockmen loosen the top layers of silage and throw it down so that the cows can reach it.

Cows need extra food, particularly during the winter, to keep up their supply of milk. This is given as *concentrates*. These are pellets prepared by feed merchants from seeds and nuts, often imported from abroad. When the cows come in to be milked they each receive some concentrates.

*Cows feeding in the silage barn*

## Farming

## Milk

Each cow must be milked twice a day, every day, summer and winter, early in the morning and again in the afternoon. This is done in the milking parlour. The cows come in, step up on to a platform and settle down to eat their concentrates. The stockman washes the udders and attaches the cups of the milking machine. The milk passes from the cows into containers. There the amount given by each cow is weighed and recorded and the milk is pumped through pipes to be cooled and stored in a large tank.

A cow does not give milk until she has had a calf. Young cows, called *heifers*, usually have their first calves when they are two or three years old. They calve between October and March and then give milk for about ten months. Then they produce another calf and come into milk again.

From about one week old the calves are taught to drink milk from a bucket and then the mother joins the milking herd. The cow calves are kept to join the herd when they are fully grown. The bull calves are sent to market and are bought by other farmers who specialize in meat production.

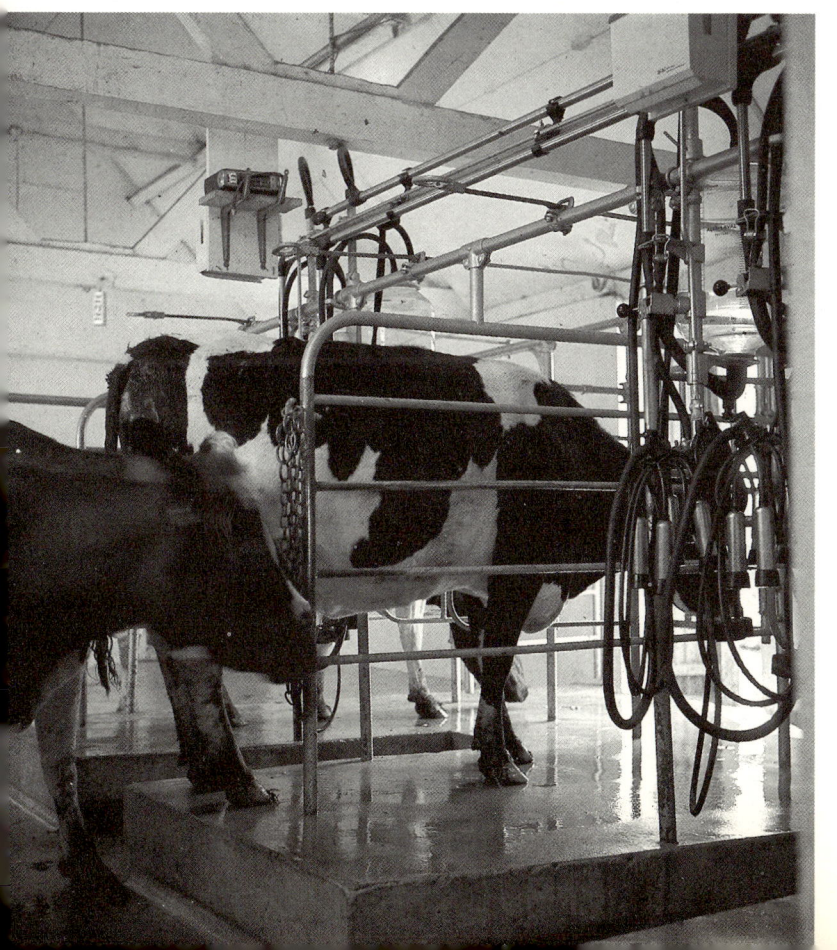

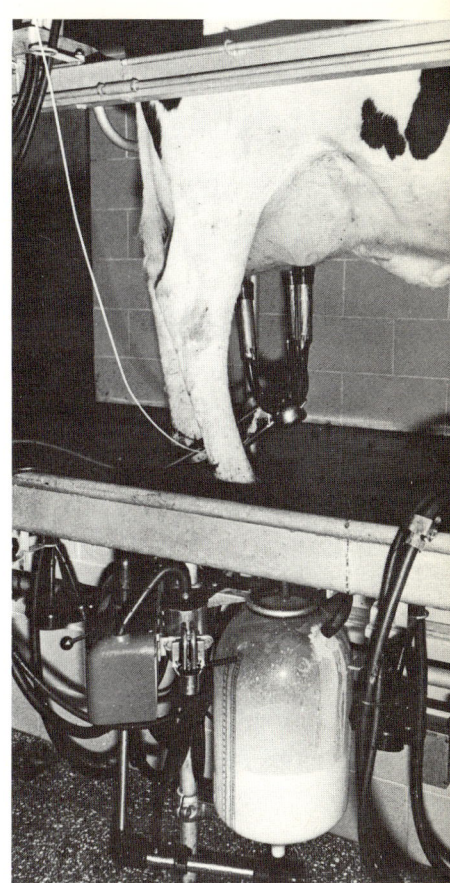

*The cups of the milking machine fit on to the cow's udder and the milk passes into a container to be weighed and recorded*

*The cows entering the milking parlour where they find food*

*Bottling milk in a big dairy*

*Making farmhouse cheese*

Once every day a tanker calls from the nearby milk depot and pumps the milk out of the farm tank. At the depot milk collected from many farms is pumped into giant tankers to be sent to London. There it is pasteurized (heated to kill any harmful germs), bottled and put into cold storage before being delivered next morning to people's homes.

The milk depots usually keep some of the liquid milk to make butter, dried milk, yoghurt and other dairy products.

**Cheese-making**

On this Somerset farm some of the milk is used to make farmhouse Cheddar cheese. It goes with milk from several other farms to a cheesemaker. The milk is poured into a great shallow bath and treated so that it separates into solid curd and watery whey. The solid curd is packed into big metal moulds, lined with cheesecloth. The moulds are then put into a cheese press which compresses the curd into a solid cheese, weighing about 25 kilograms.

The cheeses have to be stored with great care and allowed to mature. At first they taste very mild but gradually the flavour develops. Nowadays few farmers make cheese on their farms. Most cheese is made in factories.

*Farming*

# A farm in the Yorkshire Dales

Mr Wilson also keeps sheep but in very different conditions from those on the Somerset farm. Running from north to south through northern England are the Pennines. The heavy rain which falls on these hills drains away through wide open valleys, known in Yorkshire as *dales*. Many of the farms in the dales extend from flat land near the river up the valley sides to the high moorland above. On the lower land the farmers grow crops or keep dairy cattle, but the sheep are the animals which do best in hilly country.

There are many different breeds of sheep in Britain. On the Dales farms a small, tough and hardy breed is required to survive on the rather poor grazing and in the cold, wet conditions which are found on the higher parts of the farms. Mr Wilson has Swaledale sheep. They can live out for most of the year, even as high as 500 metres above sea-level.

## Different kinds of grazing

Mr Wilson's farm has four kinds of grazing for his animals. He has to move the groups of sheep and cattle about the farm so that each animal has good grass when it needs it most. He also needs to take a hay crop at the right time for winter feeding.

The small enclosed meadows on the flat land near the farmhouse and the river are used for hay and as grazing for the dairy cows. In early spring this is where the ewes are brought to have their lambs. The pastures on the lower slopes of the hill are used for the cattle and to fatten sheep for the market. To help the grass grow Mr Wilson spreads fertilizer on these fields.

*Clipping the sheep*

*A ewe and her lamb grazing on the rough grass of the open moorland high above the dale*

*A sheepdog waits for the farmer's command*

*The four types of grazing round a dales village*

*Farming*

Farther up the valley sides, where slopes become steep and often rocky, long straight stone walls divide the land into very large fields. These are rough grazing. This grass too is treated with fertilizer but, at 500 metres above sea-level, grass does not grow well and the heavy rain tends to wash the fertilizer away.

Beyond the stone wall which forms the boundary of the farm there is open moorland. This does not belong to the farm but Mr Wilson has the right to graze a fixed number of animals there. The sheep have to be trained to stay on his part of the moor. When the young lambs go up with their mothers, they soon learn not to stray, even though the moor stretches for 30 to 40 kilometres without any fences. Drivers on the narrow roads across the moor between one dale and the next have to watch out for sheep and lambs wandering across the roads.

When Mr Wilson moves his sheep from high ground to low or from low to high, he does it in stages. They need get used to the change in height above sea-level and to the difference in grazing. In moving sheep the shepherd is helped by his dogs, usually Scottish or Welsh collies. These highly trained dogs can gather a flock together, move the sheep from place to place and seek out any which have strayed. If the sheep are buried under heavy winter snow, the dogs will find them for the shepherd to rescue.

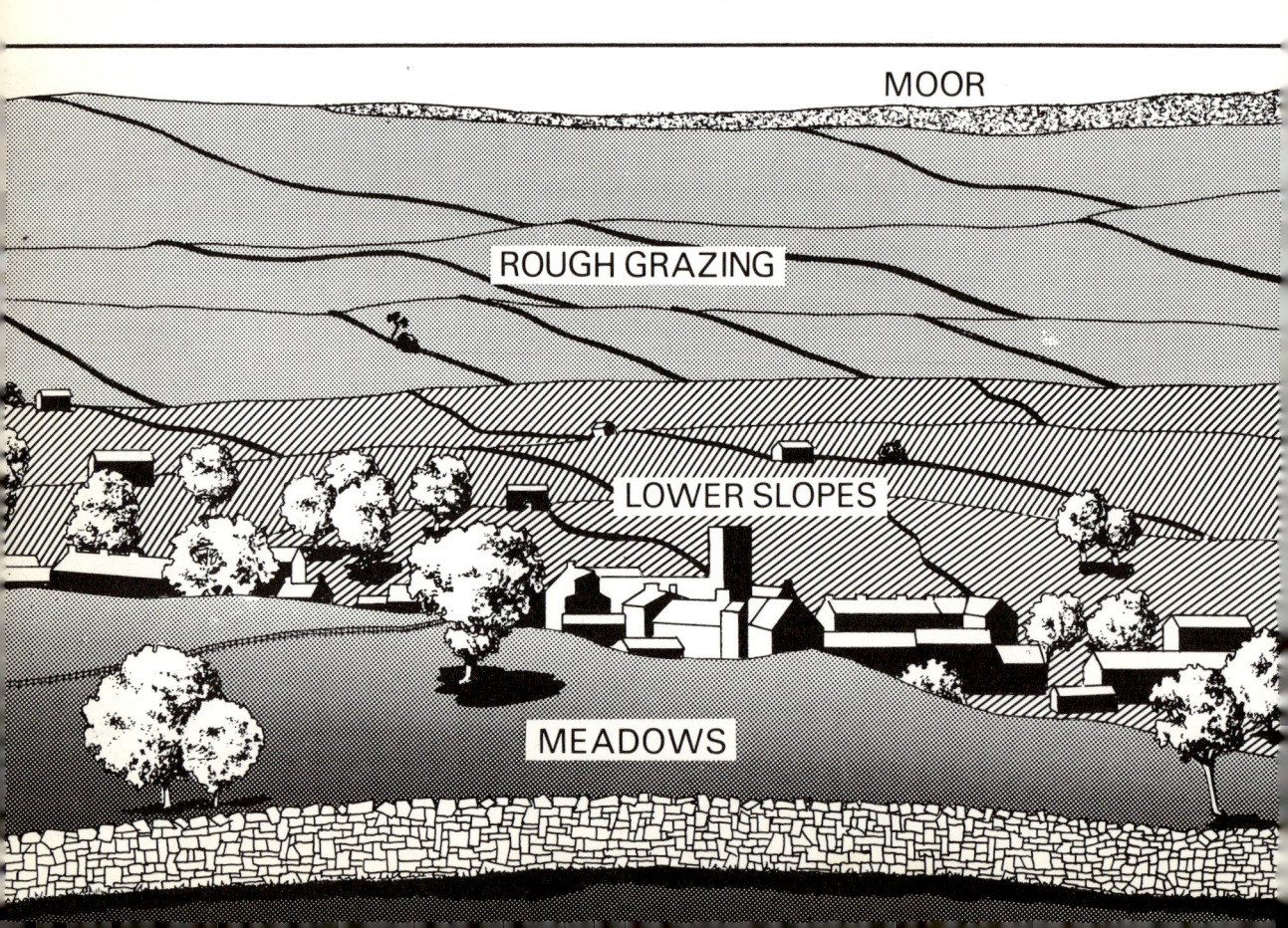

MOOR

ROUGH GRAZING

LOWER SLOPES

MEADOWS

*Gathering the sheep for clipping*

*Clipping the sheep in the shelter of a drystone wall*

## The farmer's year

In the autumn the ewes are mated ready for the annual crop of lambs. By February or March the grazing on the high moor has become rather poor and hay and concentrates have to be taken up. In early April the ewes are slowly brought down in batches to the more sheltered fields near the farmhouse.

April is a very busy month for the shepherd for as many as 200 lambs may be born to a flock of 120 ewes. Afterwards the ewes with the *gimmers* (female lambs) are moved from the lowest fields into the higher pastures. The ewes with the *tups* (male lambs) stay longer on the better pastures so that the lambs will fatten up quickly. Most of the tups will be sold to butchers in the autumn.

During June and July all the ewes have to be clipped. This is done in sheep pens which have been built against the highest stone wall. The wool is collected and sold. Swaledale wool is very good for making carpets.

*Dipping the sheep to protect them from parasites*

Twice a year, in August and again in October or November, the sheep are dipped. Each sheep has to swim through a chemical wash which will prevent attacks from flies and kill off any parasites. At the August dip the lambs which are to be sold are separated from their mothers. For a few days, until they have become used to living apart, the farm rings with their noisy calling.

When the ewes are about five years old and have lambed three times, they are sold to a farm lower down the dale. Here they are mated with Wensleydale rams and produce cross-bred lambs for meat.

C63

*Potato plants in flower*

*Ploughing after the harvest in preparation for next year's potato crop*

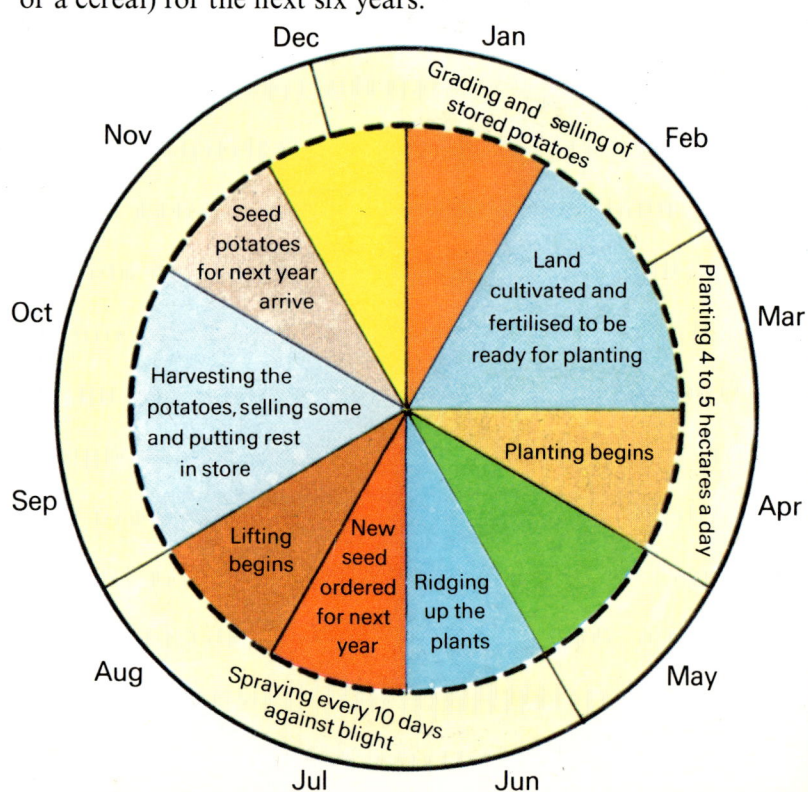

*The potato grower's year*

*Farming*

# An arable farm in Lincolnshire

Most farms grow some crops but some farms concentrate entirely on crop-growing; these are called *arable* farms. On such farms the soil needs to be easy to work and well drained. The land must be fairly flat so that heavy machinery can be used safely and so that the soil is not washed away by rain. Most important of all, there must be enough rain to keep plants growing and sunshine to ripen them for harvesting.

Crops grown on arable farms vary from farm to farm but nearly always include cereals (wheat, barley, oats), root crops (potatoes, sugar beet) and sometimes vegetables for freezing or canning (peas, beans, sprouts).

Lincolnshire is a county with many arable farms. Mr Collins has a farm of about 280 hectares on the edge of the Fens. This area has special soils which are very good for growing potatoes.

## Growing potatoes

If land is used too often for potato growing, a pest called eelworm may develop in the soil. For this reason the farmer plans carefully so that each piece of land grows potatoes one year and other crops (hay which is sold to livestock farmers, peas, beans or a cereal) for the next six years.

*The potato grower's year:*

- Jan: Grading and selling of stored potatoes
- Feb: Land cultivated and fertilised to be ready for planting
- Mar: Planting 4 to 5 hectares a day
- Apr: Planting begins
- May: Ridging up the plants
- Jun–Jul: Spraying every 10 days against blight
- Aug: New seed ordered for next year
- Sep: Lifting begins
- Oct: Harvesting the potatoes, selling some and putting rest in store
- Nov: Seed potatoes for next year arrive

*Farming*

Growing potatoes on a large scale is a round-the-year job in which machinery plays an important part. The potato-growing year begins when the previous crop has been harvested. The land is spread with manure and ploughed. Then it is left till spring.

The seed potatoes have to *chit* or sprout before they are planted. They are laid on chitting trays and placed in a glasshouse or a special chitting house. They need an even temperature of about 5°C. After five months the sprouts have formed and the potatoes are ready for planting.

As planting time grows near, the ground is *harrowed* to break up the soil into what the farmer calls "a good tilth". It is spread with fertilizer. Then a machine called a potato planter is used to drop the seed potatoes into the ground; it also puts more fertilizer on each side of them and covers them with a ridge of soil. When the plants begin to grow they are ridged up again to keep the potatoes covered. Weeds and pests have to be kept down by spraying until it is time to lift the crop.

*Trays full of seed potatoes in the chitting house*

*A potato planter at work. You can see the ridges of soil it makes to cover the potatoes*

*The potato harvester picks up the potatoes and loads them into lorries*

*Inside the potato store. Before potatoes are sold, they are graded into sizes*

Potato lifting is done by another special machine. Four or five people make up a team. One drives the harvester, while two others drive tractors and trailers which work alongside and carry the potatoes to the store. Someone else works on the machine itself. The harvester lifts the potatoes and the soil around them. X-rays are used to identify the potatoes from the clods of earth and to operate mechanical fingers to pick up the potatoes.

The potatoes are taken to the store. Some are sold at once. The rest are kept in store. Air temperature and ventilation are carefully controlled so that the potatoes keep in perfect condition for selling later.

Potato growing and selling are organized in Britain by the Potato Marketing Board which tries to ensure that farmers produce enough good-quality potatoes every year to supply the shops and for the factories which freeze, dehydrate (dry) or put the potatoes in cans or make crisps.

Before the potatoes leave the farm, they are graded. They first pass over a moving sieve. Small potatoes pass through holes in the sieve and are sold separately. Potatoes which are too big or which have been damaged are picked off a moving belt by hand and used for feeding cattle.

*Farming*

## Wheat and barley

The farmer also has to plan for his other main crops. In the autumn he prepares the soil in the fields which are to grow *winter* wheat and barley. These crops are sown in the autumn and harvested the following summer. This land also needs fertilizers which are put in at the same time as the seed. The machine which does this is a seed drill.

Wheat and barley sown in the autumn are 70 to 100 millimetres high by early spring and look like bright green grass in neat parallel rows. The fields are rolled to make sure the plants are firmly rooted. Chemicals are applied to check weeds and to prevent disease.

By August the wheat and barley are golden in colour and are harvested by combines. The grain is dried and stored until it is sold, the wheat for making flour, the barley for brewing. The straw is baled to be used to protect the potatoes in store or sold for animal bedding. Some may be burned in the fields and the ashes ploughed in.

*Harvesting barley*

## Sugar beet

Sugar beet looks like a long parsnip. The seeds are sown in drills in spring and are later "singled" or thinned out.

The sugar-beet harvest comes at the same time as the potato harvest. The heavy roots are lifted by another specialized machine, the beet harvester. The roots are taken to a factory which extracts and refines the sugar. Over 40 per cent of all the sugar we use in Britain comes from our own farms.

*A sugar beet*

*A sugar-beet harvester*

*Farming*

# Market gardening

When people go to a greengrocer or supermarket they expect to be able to buy fresh vegetables and salad crops all the year round. Some of this food may be grown by fruit growers or arable farmers who have some fields of lettuce, cabbages, beans, sprouts and cabbages. But most come from farmers who grow only vegetables. Their farms are called market gardens or vegetable farms, and they are called growers.

Most market gardens are within easy reach of a big city where there is a wholesale market for fruit and vegetables. This ensures that the produce is in good condition when it reaches the shops.

Market gardens need fertile soil which is easy to work and well drained. They must be in places where early crops are not likely to be damaged by frost.

Mr Simpson has a market garden near London. Some of the crops are grown outdoors but he also has a large area covered by glass and plastic sheeting. Within these areas the light, the temperature and the humidity (the amount of water in the air) are carefully controlled so that the plants will ripen when Mr Simpson wants them to. These houses are costly to run because they need to be heated in spring. That is why salad vegetables are so expensive in spring.

**Indoor crops**

The main crops grown in the houses are tomatoes and cucumber. Tomatoes are grown by trailing them along wires. In this way many kilograms of fruit can be raised from one plant. Cucumbers are grown in a similar way and the long straight fruit hang down from the plants. These plants require a great deal of work since at every stage each individual plant must be trained, tied, sprayed and fed. The amount of water they receive is carefully controlled to suit the stage of growth.

Such intensive cultivation requires plenty of fertilizer and sometimes soils are specially prepared to meet the needs of a particular crop. This kind of "farming" is very different from those you have already learned about, since climate and soils are both artificially controlled.

**Outdoor crops**

Outdoors Mr Simpson produces a wide variety of vegetables. These include several kinds of cabbage and sprouts for the winter and spring. He also grows early potatoes, French beans

*Picking greenhouse tomatoes*

and peas for the early summer, spring onions, radishes, courgettes, celery, peppers, large onions and, above all, lettuce. Some of these are sown indoors or in special seedbeds and then transplanted to the fields.

Early in the growing season outdoor crops may be protected by plastic cloches or tunnels.

Many market-garden crops take a fairly short time to grow so Mr Simpson has to plan carefully to make sure that the land is being fully used all the time. Sometimes small crops are planted in between others which take a little longer to grow. The first crop will be picked before the second one is ready. Sometimes one crop follows another on the same land. This happens in Thanet, Kent, where autumn cauliflowers are followed by spring cabbage.

Like most other farmers Mr Simpson saves expensive labour by using machinery. Tractors (smaller than those used on other kinds of farm) pull cultivators, seed drills and machines which can put tender young plants into the ground without damage. Spraying equipment is also needed to create a fine mist of water which settles gently on tender leaves. Pumps and piping are needed to irrigate crops when water is short.

*Packing lettuce in plastic bags*

*Growing seedlings inside a giant plastic tunnel*

*Picking celery*

*The new Covent Garden market, one of the big wholesale markets at which growers sell their produce to greengrocers*

*Bunching spring onions*

*Farming*

## Harvesting and marketing

Throughout the harvesting season, which may last from May to February, depending on what is grown, extra labour is needed. Mr Simpson employs local people who come when they are needed but do not work all the year round. They pick, cut, bunch and prepare the crops and help with the packing.

The grading, packaging and marketing of fresh vegetables are a very important part of market gardening. Large concerns often do their own but Mr Simpson belongs to a marketing association which does it for him. Mr Simpson's market garden is close enough to London for some of his produce to be sold there. Once it has been packed it is loaded on to lorries and driven overnight to reach New Covent Garden or other markets in time for selling next day.

Mr Simpson also has his own farm shop where he sells packs of vegetables. Local people also come and pick their own beans, peas, courgettes and broccoli for a lower price. This saves labour costs and people enjoy working in the open air and filling their freezers at the same time.

*Farming*

# Fruit farming in Kent

Mr Cook's fruit farm occupies about six hectares of land and is much smaller than the dairy, sheep and arable farms we have looked at. It stands in well-wooded countryside near the border between Kent and East Sussex. Compared with many parts of Britain the climate in Kent is dry and sunny, so it is good for growing fruit. Mr Cook's main crops are apples and pears, with some strawberries and raspberries.

The highest part of the farm is just over 100 metres above sea-level. The land slopes gently downwards towards the south-east. This slope allows cold air to drain away from the fruit trees. This is important because spring frosts are the enemy of the fruit farmer. The soil is a silty loam which is very suitable for fruit.

Although the farm is small, growing fruit is a very demanding job and keeps the farmer busy all the year. The trees must be sprayed to avoid loss from pests and diseases. This is done several times during the winter and *once a week* from April to July. Pruning begins in November and goes on continually until early April. All pruning is done by hand. Young trees must be pruned to grow into the correct shape and older trees to provide plenty of air and light for the fruit buds.

Because Mr Cook has so many trees growing close together, he must keep the soil in good condition by putting down fertilizer in autumn and again in spring.

*Pruning apple trees in winter*

*Spraying takes place all the year round*

*Farming*

**Planning the orchard**

Fruit trees, once established, give the farmer an annual crop of fruit for fifteen to twenty years. After that the yield grows less, so the trees are grubbed up and a new orchard planted. The farmer plans his planting so that only a part of the orchards have to be replanted in any one year.

The root part or rootstock of most fruit trees is of a different variety from the top flowering and fruiting part. Cuttings of the variety wanted are grafted or joined to a specially grown rootstock which has good roots and is stronger than the variety's own rootstock. The size of the fully-grown tree depends on the type of rootstock chosen. One type of rootstock will produce a tree twice as tall as that grown on another.

The older trees in the orchard are tall and stand about 7 metres apart. But, as these are grubbed out, trees grafted on to a dwarf rootstock are being planted. These new trees are planted in straight lines about 2 metres apart. Every young tree is carefully staked so that it stands firm against the wind until its roots are well established. The trees are trained so that they do not grow more than about 2.5 metres high. This means that the trees can be pruned and the fruit picked without the use of long ladders.

The farmer has to plan what varieties to grow to meet the demands of the market. He needs fruit that can be sold during the autumn months; and fruit that will keep well and keep the markets supplied during the winter.

Many fruit trees will not fruit unless their flowers receive pollen from a different variety, so Mr Cook has to be careful which varieties he chooses to grow.

*A young apple tree. You can see how a cutting has been grafted on to a rootstock of a different variety*

*The orchard in winter*

*Blossom-time*

*The strawberries are picked straight into punnets*

*Apple picking begins in August and carries on until the end of October. (Different kinds of apple ripen at different times.)*

## Strawberries

The strawberries are grown in three different ways. Some are protected by glass or polythene, so that they will ripen earlier. (This is done in February or in early March.) The rest are left unprotected. Like the orchards the strawberry beds must be fertilized and sprayed against diseases and pests. Picking begins in mid-May when prices are high and continues until the middle of July. The strawberries are picked into punnets with very great care so that they reach the customer in perfect condition. If the weather is right there may be a second crop towards the end of August.

## Apple picking

Apple picking begins in the first week in August with an early cooking apple. At this busy time extra help is needed, so local people and students on holiday come in to help.

*Checking the weight of boxes of fruit before they are sent to market*

*Taking fruit into the controlled-atmosphere store*

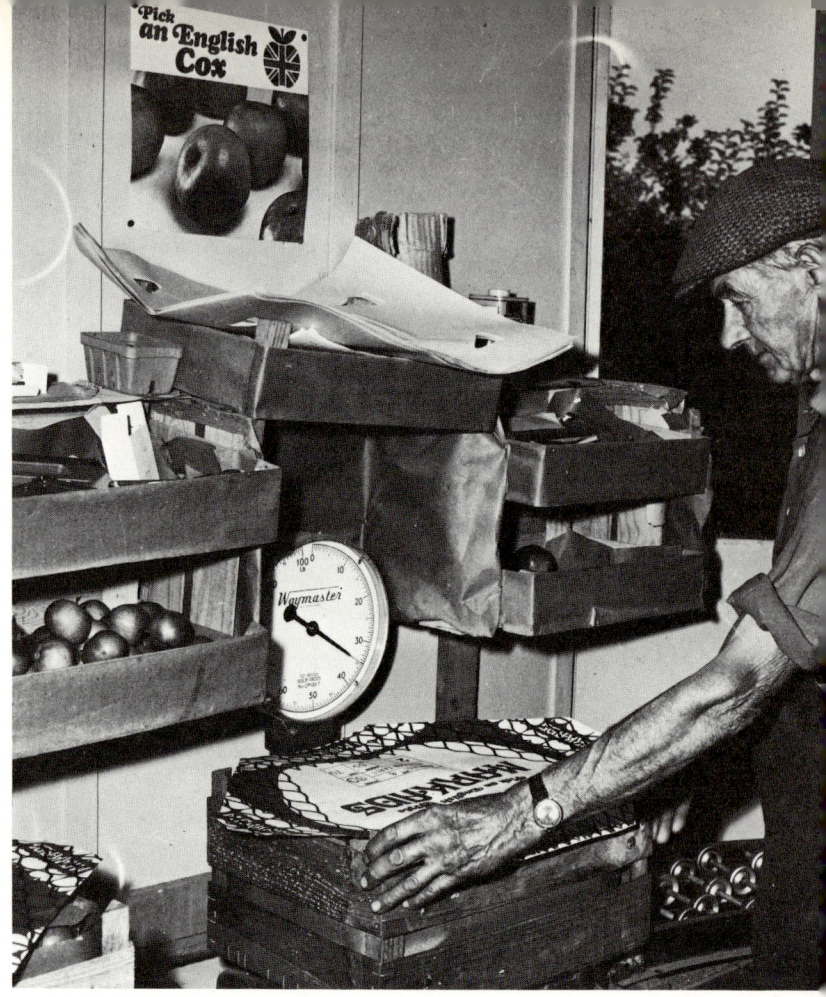

The picked fruit is taken in large boxes to the packhouse where it is cleaned, graded into sizes by machines and hand-packed into boxes.

Some fruit is sold straightaway but the rest is stored to be sold during the winter and early spring. The farm has two controlled-atmosphere (CA) stores, each of which can house about 35 tonnes of fruit. Here the fruit is kept just above freezing point with the right amount of oxygen to prevent the fruit from ripening and to ensure that it remains in good condition when it is taken out of store.

**Selling the fruit**

Like Mr Simpson, the market gardener, Mr Cook belongs to a co-operative marketing association. The association collects the fruit from the farm and arranges to sell it.

Mr Cook's farm borders a main road so he has his own shop. Here he sells apples, pears, strawberries and raspberries direct to the public. Every spring he also invites his customers to visit the farm to see the fruit trees in blossom.

*Farming*

# British farming today

You now know something about five different kinds of farming, but farming is a complicated business and there are many other kinds of farms. Some farmers grow arable crops *and* keep animals; others live in hilly country and keep cattle for meat rather than for milk. Some grow animal feeding stuffs and also breed pigs or keep thousands of poultry for eggs and meat. Farms differ from each other because every farmer makes his living by producing the best he can on his own particular farm.

Until about forty years ago most farmers in Britain had what were known as mixed farms; this meant that they did a bit of everything. Nowadays most farmers specialize in one or two kinds of farming about which they have special knowledge. Research is always going on to improve breeds of plants and animals, machinery is always being improved or invented to do special jobs and there is increasing knowledge about ways of controlling pests and diseases. So farmers are always changing and experimenting with new methods.

In spite of this it is still possible to look at Britain as a whole and see some areas where one particular kind of farming activity is more important than any other. The main arable farms are found in the east, in the Midlands and the south of England. Most of our animal farms are in the western parts of Britain. Farming which needs special conditions of climate or soil does not fit into this general pattern but occurs in places which can provide these. But it is important to remember as you travel about Britain that you will see many farms on which farmers have worked out their own particular farming policy.

■ Hill farming and stock rearing
□ Dairying
▨ Cropping with livestock
▦ Potatoes, sugar beet, vegetables, pigs, poultry and fruit

*Types of farming in Britain*

*Using an ultrasonic device to measure the depth of fat on a pig*

*Beef cattle*

# Fishing

*The types of fish found around Britain*

*An inshore boat and its catch*

Britain is surrounded by shallow seas. In these seas fish thrive because there is plenty of food for them to eat—smaller fish or plankton (tiny sea creatures and plants). In the past much of the North Sea and many parts of Britain's coastal waters were overfished. Today vessels are only allowed to catch fixed amounts of certain types of fish. This allows the fish to spawn and the sea to be restocked. Fishermen also use nets which let the small fish escape through the net.

The map shows the main fishing grounds in the seas around Britain. A trawler skipper often has fish-finding equipment to help him find the shoals: the sonar shows where the fish are swimming ahead of the ship, and a dark shadow on the screen of the echo-sounder tells him when he is towing his net through a shoal of fish.

Some of the fish, such as cod, haddock, plaice and sole, live near the bottom of the sea where they find their food. Other fish, such as sprats, herring and mackerel, live and feed near the surface.

## Inshore fishing

More than half of Britain's fish is caught by a fleet of several thousand inshore boats. These boats, which are up to 25 metres long, go out from ports all round our coast. Their voyages last from a few hours to two or three days. Inshore fishermen catch sprats and mackerel, coley (saithe), whiting, dabs and plaice, crabs, prawns, cockles and mussels.

Distant water freezer stern trawler

Distant water side trawler

Middle and near water trawler

Inshore fishing vessel

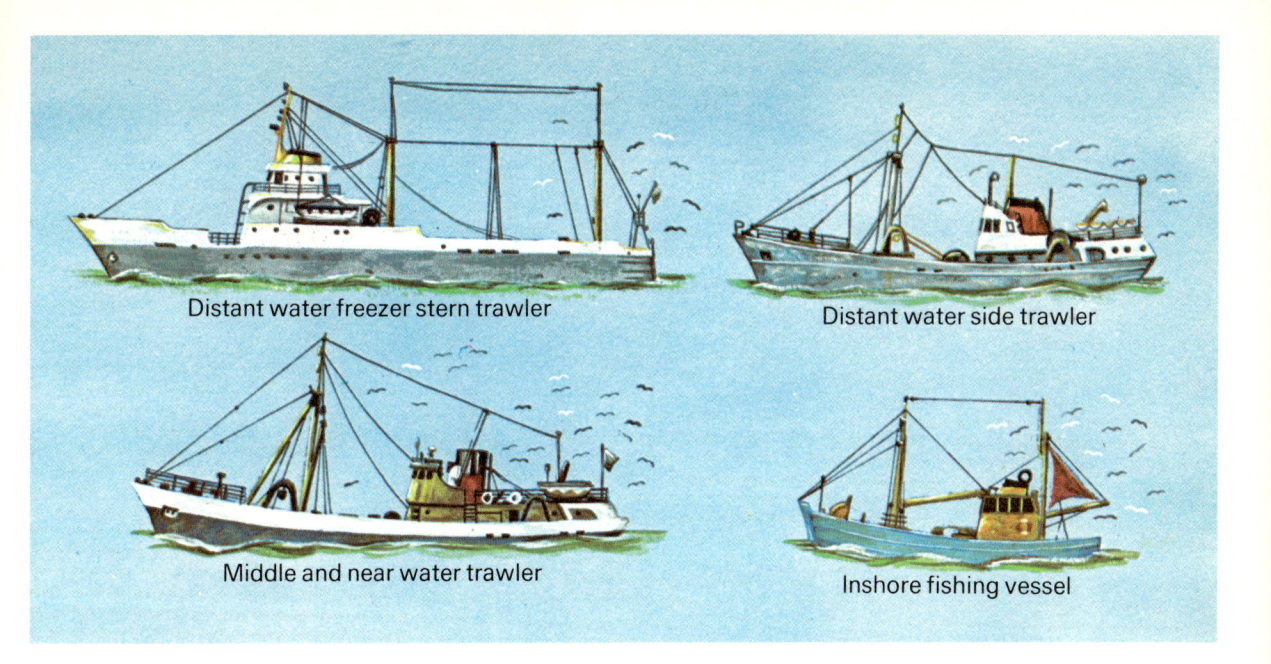

## Near and middle-water vessels

Near-water and middle-water vessels are larger than the inshore boats. These trawlers are at sea for about three days to a week (depending on their size) and they often meet icy seas and stormy weather. They fish in the North Sea, in the Atlantic off the north-west coast of Britain and in the Minch (a stretch of water between the Outer Hebrides and the Scottish mainland).

The crew gut and wash the white fish and pack it in ice in boxes. Larger trawlers store the catch in a fish hold packed between layers of ice.

## Distant-water trawlers

These are the giants of the fishing fleet and many of them have a crew of twenty or more. They are often called *stern trawlers* because they "shoot" their nets from the stern. Some of the trawlers are big factory ships which freeze the whole of their catch at sea within a few hours of hauling in their nets.

Britain's distant-water trawlers used to sail for many days to reach fishing grounds round Iceland but now these waters are open only to Icelandic trawlers. Every year the deep-sea fleet is getting smaller and the ships have few places to go to and very little to catch. Some of the big trawlers from the Humber and the Scottish ports now fish for mackerel off the coast of Cornwall. The local fishermen are worried that the mackerel, like the herring, may be overfished. In a day's catch a stern trawler, with its huge net, can pull in about eighteen times more mackerel than a fisherman working from an inshore boat.

*Types of fishing vessel*

*Trawlers in port*

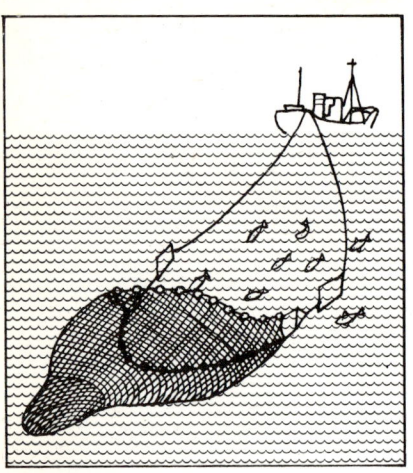

*An otter trawl*

*A stern trawler. The trawl is hauled up the ramp in the stern*

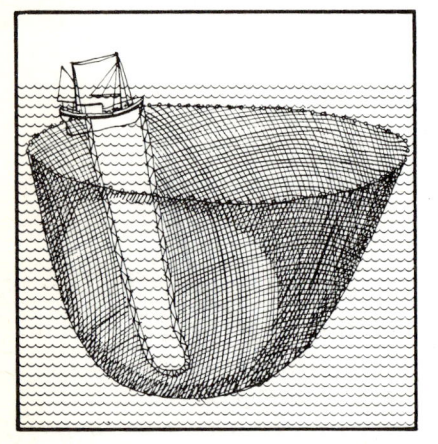

*Purse seining*

*On the bridge of a trawler*

## Purse seining

Fish such as herring, mackerel and sprats—which swim near the surface—are caught mainly with a purse seine net. One end is thrown over the side and attached to a buoy. Then the purse seiner circles the shoal, paying out the net as she goes. When the boat returns to the buoy the purse strings are pulled to close the bottom of the net so that the fish cannot escape. The net is usually hauled aboard. Some purse seine vessels, however, pump the catch from the sea into the hold. A purse seine net can cover a stretch of water larger than a football field. It is stored on a special drum on the deck.

## Bottom trawl: otter trawl nets

Fish which live on or near the seabed are caught in a bottom trawl net. This net has rollers along the bottom and, as it is towed over the seabed, the "mouth" is kept open by two otter boards (or doors). The fish swim into the main part of the net and then go through a small opening into the cod end (the tail end which holds the catch). The fish are unable to escape from the cod end and, after three hours' trawling, the net is winched up a ramp in the stern. The rope at the cod end is untied and the fish go down a chute on to the working deck. Here they are gutted, washed, packed in ice or frozen into 40-kilogram blocks.

An otter trawl net can also be used for mid-water fishing where herring, mackerel and sprats are caught. When it is used in mid water the net has floats along the top to keep it from sinking towards the seabed. Some of the fishing boats fish with purse seine nets as well as with trawl nets. They are called multi-purpose vessels.

*Fishing*

## Finding other sources of fish

Freezer trawlers used to fish for cod and haddock in Icelandic waters but this has now been ended. Some freezer trawlers are now bringing in other kinds of fish. One of these is *blue whiting*. This tiny fish (10-30 centimetres long) swims in dense shoals and in a few minutes a skipper can fill his net with vast loads. Blue whiting must be frozen within an hour, otherwise it will not stay fresh. It can be mixed with fish such as cod, hake and coley and used to make fish fingers and fish cakes.

## Landing and selling the fish

At the ports the fish is auctioned at a quayside market. Some of the fish which is caught by the freezer vessels is "quick-frozen" and stored in a refrigerated warehouse until it is needed. Then, when the seas are stormy and the boats cannot leave harbour, there is always a reserve of frozen fish for the fish-monger and for the fried-fish shops.

Fish also goes from the ports to nearby freezer factories. Here whole fish such as plaice are packed ready for selling to the supermarkets, and other fish is processed into fish steaks and fish fingers. Refrigerated and insulated lorries take some of the catch to markets in the big cities.

*Landing the fish*

*Packing fish into a plate freezer in a frozen-foods factory*

*The fish is auctioned on the quayside*

*Fishing*

### Preserving fish

There are many ways of preserving fish. Herrings are split, gutted, washed and hung in the smoke from chestnut or oak wood-shavings to make kippers. Now that there is a shortage of cod and herring, more mackerel are being preserved. They can be smoked like herring, pickled in vinegar and spices and canned in brine, oil or tomato sauce.

Most of the fish caught round the shores of Britain is sold for eating. However, small amounts of sand-eels and mackerel and the heads and bones of fish such as cod are dried and powdered to make animal food and fertilizer. Oil is also extracted from the cod's liver to make cod-liver oil.

### Fish farming

Fish such as turbot and Dover sole are in short supply in the seas round Britain. These fish are expensive to buy as only small amounts are caught. In several places in Britain, particularly off the west coast of Scotland, where there is less pollution in the sea, fish farms have been started. When the young fish reach a certain size, they are fattened in onshore tanks, often in heated water pumped from coastal power stations, or are put into cages in the sea. There are also trout farms and farms for the breeding of salmon.

At the moment, although only a very small amount of the fish sold in Britain is farmed, there are plans to increase the sea-fish farm harvest. Fish farming will help to conserve those species of fish which are in short supply in our seas.

*Preparing fish for smoking*

*Hanging mackerel for smoking*

*Feeding sea fish in cages at a fish farm in a Scottish sea loch*

# Transport

We have been looking at industry and agriculture and some of the things they produce. But none of these manufacturers or producers could work without good systems of transport, by land, air and sea, and without good communications (by post and telephone).

Here are some of the different forms of transport and communication used by a big Leicester company which makes clothing for chain stores all over the country. You can see that the production of even one sweater depends upon a complex network of transport and communications.

*Some of the transport and communications used by a factory in Leicester*

### INSIDE THE FACTORY

Wheelers and electric motors.

Fork lift trucks.

Conveyor belt moves goods between machines.

Factory has its own telephone directory – it has so many telephones!

Newsheets, etc., to keep workforce informed of what is going on in the company.

### OUTSIDE THE FACTORY: IN BRITAIN

Raw materials brought in – yarn, etc., semi-finished goods taken to other Corah factories for finishing.

Goods out to customers, big stores throughout Britain.

Sales people to customers.

Red Star Parcels for small parcels and samples to customers in a hurry.

Post – inquiries, orders, etc.

Inquiries, orders, etc.

### OUTSIDE THE FACTORY: ABROAD

Sales people to Europe

Concorde: Sales executives to U.S.A.

Corah exports and sales people to Canada.

Corah exports to Europe: e.g. France, Germany, Scandinavia.

Orders, queries, general communications to Europe, Canada and other countries.

*Transport*

# Road

Road transport plays a vital part in Britain's economy. It moves both people and goods. There is a road of some kind to even the remotest farm or hamlet, and many towns have no railway station and so depend on road transport.

Road can be the cheapest form of passenger transport but it is often the slowest because roads may be narrow and crowded. Motorways—fast dual-carriageway roads—make road journeys between major cities in Britain very much quicker. You can travel from London to Glasgow, 634 kilometres, entirely on dual carriageway.

About 85 per cent of all goods are moved by road. Some companies have their own fleets of special vehicles—chemical companies and cement works have their own tankers, the National Coal Board uses enormous tip-up trucks and frozen-food companies have their own refrigerated trucks. Other companies hire special vehicles when they need them: car transporters or huge vans with hanging rails for clothing.

Haulage companies provide a transport service for manufacturers. Some provide regular services which cover most routes in Britain and can in some cases even guarantee delivery of goods within a certain time limit.

Some carriers connect with land and sea services too. They deliver to wharfs and docks at British ports and to airports. They have their own depots and staff there who clear goods through Customs.

A big haulage company based in Leicester, for instance, provides transport within Britain and into Europe for manufacturers in the Midlands. Regular loads include fork-lift trucks, steel tubes, tyres and yarn—products which are typical of the Midlands.

This Leicester haulier carries goods mainly to British ports such as Tilbury, Hull, Liverpool, Southampton and others. Some loads or part loads go to industries near the ports and some to the actual ports for export. The heavy lorries (30 tonnes when loaded) use motorway routes like the M5 to South Wales ports and Bristol and the M6 to Liverpool and Scotland.

Lorry drivers drop off their load at the destination and, if they are more than 320 kilometres from Leicester, they are then told where to pick up a return load or "backload". If they are less than 320 kilometres from Leicester, it is cheaper to return with an empty truck because the cost of reloading for a short journey is too great.

*Heavy traffic in a city street*

*Transferring containers from rail to road transport*

*Motorways connect the main industrial areas of Britain*

*Transport*

# Rail

Railways are important for carrying both passengers and goods. Rail travel is particularly attractive for short journeys for passengers into and out of cities (commuters) and for long distances between major cities (Inter-City travel). Commuters are people who travel daily into cities to work. Over a quarter of a million commuters arrive each morning at the London railway stations of Waterloo, Liverpool Street, Victoria, London Bridge and Charing Cross.

Rail can provide an important service within a city too. London and Glasgow have underground railway systems. Existing railways in Tyneside are being linked by new bridges and tunnels to give the area a new rapid transport system.

British Rail has a network of fast Inter-City expresses between main cities. On some lines they run High Speed Trains (HST), trains with powerful streamlined engines at each end. On the run between London and Bristol the Inter-City 125 averages over 125 miles (160 kilometres) an hour.

British Rail has an even more exciting train, the Advanced Passenger Train (APT). The power car for the APT has a top speed of over 250 kilometres an hour. The coaches of these supertrains are designed to tilt so that they can go round bends at high speeds without making their passengers uncomfortable. On the London to Glasgow line the APT cuts the journey time to just over four hours.

*Glasgow's new Metro underground railway*

*An Inter-City express*

*The Advanced Passenger Train (APT)*

## Transport

British Rail has streamlined its freight services. Speedlink is a service of freight trains, running to a regular timetable between the major cities. There are about fifty trains every twenty-four hours, mostly travelling at night. Speedlink moves steel between South Wales and Glasgow and whisky in bulk from Scotland for export to Europe. Speedlink has connections with the European freight network through the Dover and Harwich train ferries.

Some goods are carried in containers, large boxes of wood and steel designed to fit on to special lorries and railway wagons and to be carried in specially designed ships. Containers can be transferred easily from rail into ships or on to lorries without the goods inside being unloaded. British Rail's container service is called Freightliner. It has container terminals with large sidings and huge cranes at Stratford in London and at Ipswich, for instance.

British Rail moves all sorts of goods and commodities: coal, iron and steel, oil and chemicals, building materials, food and drink, agricultural produce and motor vehicles. Many of these need specially designed wagons—tankers, car transporters, refrigerated trucks and so on. Some wagons have the company's name on them. You have probably seen some of these.

*Loading parcels on to a passenger train*

*The freight terminal at Dover*

*A car transporter*

*Some companies have their own rail tankers*

*A triple-headed iron ore train*

Aviation fuel is moved by rail from the oil refinery at Fawley, near Southampton, to Prestwick Airport, near Glasgow. British Rail also carries oil from Humberside to the oil-fired power stations in the Midlands.

Rail is a good way of moving very heavy loads. To encourage industries to transport their goods by rail the government helps them by granting money to help pay for railway wagons and for the building of railway sidings.

Some of the heaviest trains are the iron-ore trains, carrying ore from the Welsh ports to the steelworks inland. The iron-ore trains between Port Talbot and Llanwern in South Wales weigh over 3000 tonnes. They are triple-headed trains; that is, they are pulled by three locomotives.

*A "merry-go-round" train carrying coal to a power station*

Power stations which need regular supplies of coal in bulk are served by trains of wagons, permanently coupled together, which are loaded and unloaded automatically as they move round a circular track. At the coal mine the wagons are filled with coal. When the train reaches the power station, it travels slowly round another circular track. As the wagons reach the unloading point, doors in the bottom of the wagons open and the coal drops on to conveyor belts which carry it to the power station. The train continues round the track, without stopping, and travels back to the coal mine for another load. This is called a "merry-go-round" system.

British Rail keeps track of all its goods trains and wagons by using a computer. The computer records and reports on every detail of freight traffic throughout the British Rail network and even into France. This computerized system of keeping track of wagons is called TOPS (Total Operations Processing System).

*Transport*

# Air

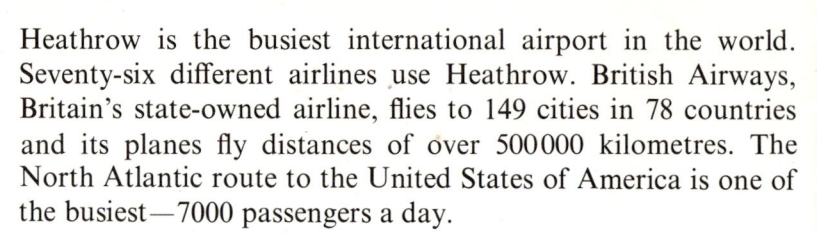

Heathrow is the busiest international airport in the world. Seventy-six different airlines use Heathrow. British Airways, Britain's state-owned airline, flies to 149 cities in 78 countries and its planes fly distances of over 500 000 kilometres. The North Atlantic route to the United States of America is one of the busiest—7000 passengers a day.

In Britain British Airways operates a thousand flights a week to 26 towns and cities. On some domestic flights (flights within Britain) BA run a shuttle service on which no advance booking is needed. You can fly this way to Glasgow, Edinburgh and Belfast and possibly, in the future, also to Paris, Amsterdam and Dublin. One of the independent airlines runs a sort of shuttle service too. Laker Airlines' Skytrain to the United States also works rather like a shuttle.

Independent airlines such as British Caledonian have international services, chiefly to South America and parts of Africa, and domestic flights. Other companies operate domestic services, cross-Channel flights linked to train and coach services and charter flights of all kinds, particularly for holiday makers.

Heathrow and Gatwick airports are linked by a helicopter service. Helicopters also play an important part in the North Sea oil and gas industry.

Airlines use different types of aircraft for different routes. On heavily used long-distance routes British Airways is building up a fleet of Boeing 747 "Jumbos" with Rolls-Royce RB211 engines. For other routes the Lockheed TriStar 500 is used; this is also a wide-bodied aircraft but smaller than a Jumbo.

Concorde, the world's first supersonic aircraft (see page 30), travels faster than a rifle bullet. It cruises at over 2000 kilometres an hour and at twice the height of Mount Everest (over 16 kilometres above the earth)—well above any disturbances in the atmosphere.

Concorde flies to Washington, New York, Bahrein and Singapore and in the future may fly to Tokyo. Can you think why these cities have been chosen?

*TriStar 500*

*Boeing 747*

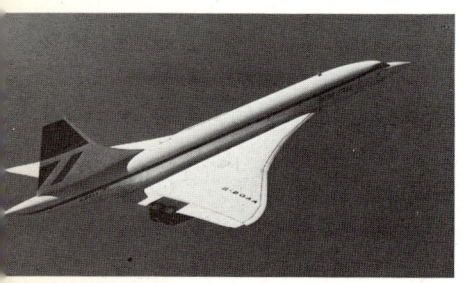

*Concorde*

*British Airways also provides a helicopter service to North Sea oil rigs*

*Loading freight on to a cargo aircraft*

## Air freight

British Airways and other British airlines carry freight, on services timetabled like passenger flights, to many cities in Europe, the United States, Canada, the Near and Far East and Australia. British Airways' Cargocentre at Heathrow can handle 3000 tonnes of exports from Britain each week and the same amount of imports. Eighty-five per cent of all British Airways cargo is handled at Cargocentre.

All sorts of cargo are carried by air, from gold and diamonds to live animals for zoos. Usually air cargo consists of goods which are valuable and light in weight or which are required very urgently.

## Local airports

Most major cities in Britain have a local airport. These are sometimes quite small and are used mainly for charter flights. Leicester, Nottingham and Derby are cities in the East Midlands. Their local airport is the East Midlands Airport at Castle Donington. Various tour operators use this airport for services to holiday areas in Europe and the Mediterranean. There are cargo services at Castle Donington too. For example, an American airline, Trans International Airlines (TIA) flies out Rolls-Royce RB 211 engines from Britain to California for use in the Lockheed TriStar. Each TIA flight from Castle Donington delivers another three RB 211s from the Rolls-Royce works at Derby.

*Cattle being exported by air from the East Midlands Airport*

*A container lorry driving on to a RORO vessel at London docks*

*A jetfoil service that links central London to Zeebrugge in Belgium*

## Crossing the Channel and the North Sea

Britain is now a member of the Common Market—this means that there are now very close trade links with the countries of Western Europe. So it is important that people and goods should be able to travel easily between Britain and Europe. Although the English Channel is only about 35 kilometres wide, crossing it is a major obstacle. People in a hurry take a plane; ferries carry passengers and cars between the Channel ports, often linking up with train services on both sides. Hovercraft provide similar services and hydrofoils too are cutting the journey time between Britain and the Continent.

People can transfer from shore to ship on their own feet but goods cannot, so goods at ports are handled by machines. Some are packed in containers which can be transferred from lorry or train to ship by giant gantry cranes. Large vehicles can easily drive on and off specially designed ships (Roll-On-Roll-Off—RORO).

*Transport*

# Transport and the environment

Moving people and goods, particularly by road, creates problems: traffic jams, air pollution from exhaust fumes, risk from dangerous loads. It is better for the environment (the surroundings in which we live) for bulky goods to travel by rail since one train can take about forty lorry loads.

Most quarrying companies use rail as well as road transport. One Leicestershire quarry transports granite to the rail sidings by a series of enclosed and almost silent conveyors nearly two kilometres long.

Canal transport is still occasionally used. Coal is delivered by barge to the Ferrybridge C power station in East Yorkshire. The barges pick the coal up from the waterside collieries and at the power station the coal is unloaded by giant tippler.

In Scotland where British Petroleum is building oil rigs, heavy equipment cannot be delivered to the coastal sites because the Scottish roads are too narrow. Instead BP uses sea barges and runs them up on to the beach.

Pipelines are used to transport some materials—cement, for example—and chemical works often use pipelines to move chemicals from the manufacturing plant to the docks nearby.

Dangerous cargoes are carried by road, rail and air. All dangerous cargoes carry warning labels and there are international codes which, when decoded, inform firemen and other services what action they should take if there is an accident.

*Barges delivering coal to Doncaster power station on the South Yorkshire Canal*

*Warning label on a road tanker*

*Some of the labels used on cargoes of chemicals*

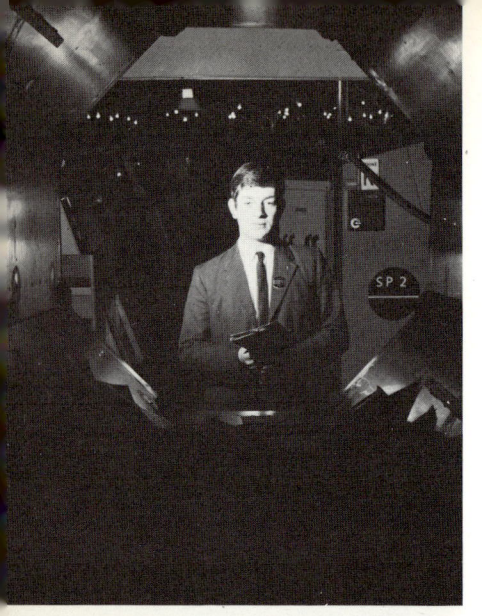

# Communications

Business, commerce and government could not work without ways of sending messages, orders, reports, accounts and information. The most important of these are provided by the Post Office.

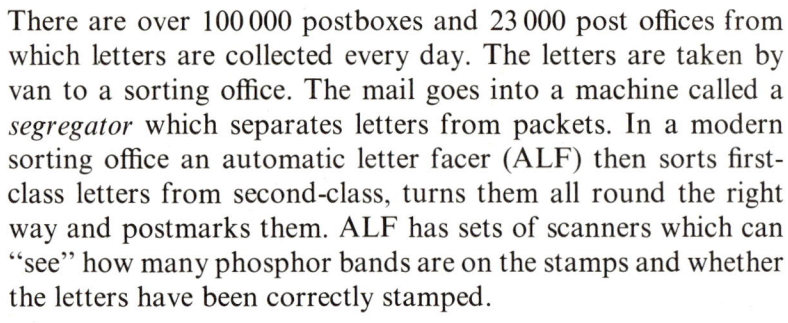

## Post

There are over 100 000 postboxes and 23 000 post offices from which letters are collected every day. The letters are taken by van to a sorting office. The mail goes into a machine called a *segregator* which separates letters from packets. In a modern sorting office an automatic letter facer (ALF) then sorts first-class letters from second-class, turns them all round the right way and postmarks them. ALF has sets of scanners which can "see" how many phosphor bands are on the stamps and whether the letters have been correctly stamped.

In a fully automated post office postcodes are very important. After ALF has sorted the letters, they go to a coding desk. A postman reads the postcode on each envelope and taps it out on the keyboard of a machine which prints the code on the letter in phosphor dots. Modern sorting machines can read phosphor dots.

Let's look at a letter with a postcode LE2 2RD, posted in London. A machine in London would be programmed to send letters postcoded "LE" to Leicester. Once the letter arrived in Leicester an automatic machine would "read" the rest of the postcode and find out which road in Leicester the letter was addressed to.

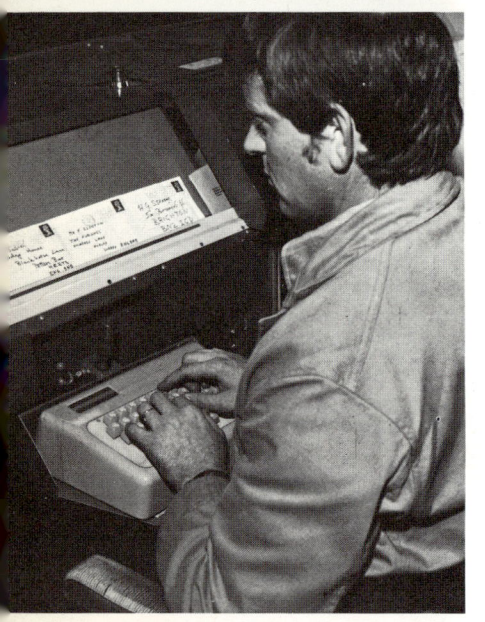

*Sorting letters. (Top) As the drum of the segregator revolves, the heavy packages drop to the bottom. (Middle) The postcode is printed on to each letter in phosphor dots. (Bottom) An automatic sorting machine reads the dots and sorts the letters*

*The Post Office's underground railway in London*

Mail is carried by different forms of transport, by road, rail, sea and air. Most letters to addresses abroad are sent by air but less urgent mail and bulky packages are sent by sea, usually in container ships.

Moving letters across London has always been difficult. London's offices produce enormous quantities of mail each day and London's roads are crowded. So the Post Office has its own underground railway with 10 kilometres of track, linking six main sorting offices and two main-line stations, Liverpool Street and Paddington.

## Telecommunications

Using the telephone we can now obtain most numbers in Britain by STD (Subscriber Trunk Dialling). In most larger towns it is possible to dial direct to more than four-fifths of the world's telephones. There is, however, a big problem. When it is 1 p.m. in London, it is 5 a.m. in San Francisco, 8 a.m. in New York, 10 p.m. in Tokyo and midnight in New Zealand. Business people in Britain are just starting work when their customers in Australia have gone home for the day. This is one reason why the *Telex* service is useful.

*As a secretary (above) types on a Telex machine, the message is instantly typed out by the customer's Telex machine (below)—inside Britain or overseas*

Each Telex subscriber has a machine called a *teleprinter*. This has a dial like a telephone and a keyboard like a typewriter. It is linked by cable, like a telephone, to a Telex exchange and through the exchange to other teleprinters in Britain and abroad.

When a firm in London wants to contact a customer in Tokyo, the operator dials the Tokyo customer's Telex number and then types out the message. Immediately in Tokyo the customer's teleprinter types out the message on to a roll of paper. Even if the Japanese office is closed, the message will be waiting when the office reopens next morning.

*Using a radiophone*

*Prestel links a television screen to a computer's store of information*

*Confravision enables people in different places to talk to and see each other*

## Communications

The Post Office also provides some very specialized services. *Radiophone*, for example, enables business people to receive and make telephone calls in their cars. *Confravision* links people in different places by sound and vision. They can see each other on a television screen as well as hear each other's voices.

"Viewdata" services are a recent development. *Ceefax* and *Oracle* provide a programme of useful information (weather forecasts, Stock Exchange prices, newsflashes) which is brought up to date regularly, sometimes every hour. This information is received on the screen of a television set which has been fitted with special equipment. When the viewer switches on the system an index of the information available appears on the screen. The viewer chooses the subject he wants and its reference number and presses the number buttons on a keypad (rather like a pocket calculator). The information he wants to consult then appears on the screen.

Prestel also uses the same keypad and a television set, but the set is linked to a telephone. When the Prestel number is dialled, the television set is linked to the Prestel computer which can hold a vast store of information. Once again the viewer uses the keypad to find the precise information he wants. In the future it may be that professional men and women such as doctors and lawyers will depend on Prestel for the up-to-date information they now obtain from reference books and journals.

Facsimile Transmission (FAX) is a way of sending information rapidly over long or short distances, using a special copying machine. A drawing or document placed in a Fax machine in London will appear on a machine in New York or Tokyo 30 seconds later.

# Changing Britain

In this book we have been looking at some of Britain's industries, its energy resources, its farming and its transport and communications. In all of them changes are taking place. New equipment requires fewer workers to operate it. Out-of-date plants close down and leave empty buildings and sites behind them.

These changes create problems for Britain. Let's look at them in detail in the setting of the Port of London.

In the big picture you can see a recent view of the Upper Docks on the river Thames. In the left half of the picture are the India Docks, opened in 1802 to handle cargoes from the West Indies. Now however few ships are using the docks. The small picture shows the Royal Docks nearby when they were very busy.

*A photograph of the Royal Docks as they used to be*

*Changing Britain*

In fact the Port of London is as busy as ever it was but it is doing much of its work in a different part of the river. Ships are expensive to run, so owners are reluctant to allow them to spend time sailing up the Thames. They prefer to use London's Tilbury Docks, the bulk terminals and the other riverside installations downstream below London.

New types of ships are being used: huge container ships, RORO vessels (see page 88), tankers, bulk carriers and combination vessels which take containers and vehicles. These all need special terminals designed for their use alone. The giant Tilbury Grain Terminal, for instance, can unload grain at the rate of 2000 tonnes an hour. The grain is delivered direct to road, rail or water transport or to the grain and flour mills which stand close by.

*The Tilbury grain terminal*

Throughout the docks and riverside human muscle is being replaced by machinery. The number of dockers has been cut from 30 000 to 7500, yet the same amount of cargo is being handled. In some cases the traffic has increased. The timber terminal at Tilbury handles more than twice as much wood and other forest products as its forerunner, the old Surrey Docks, ever did, but uses only half the space.

*The container terminal at Tilbury*

*Wine is stored in tanks at the bulk wine berth*

*It is carried to the wine companies in road tankers*

Some new uses have been found for the older docks. Wine used to be imported in barrels and stored in underground cellars. Now much of it is piped ashore from tankers to a bulk wine terminal in the India Docks.

While the Port of London's activities are being moved down river, the old docks remain. What is to happen to them and to the people whose lives are centred on them? Are the people who lose their jobs, if further docks close, to move away from the area to find new homes and work elsewhere?

This is a problem that is occurring all over Britain as patterns of industry and trade change. When an old-fashioned steelworks or a coal pit closes, a whole town may suffer because people lose their jobs. If new industry is set up, it may solve only part of the problem because new factories are designed so that machines do most of the work. Few workers are needed and their work will be very different from that of steelworks or coal mine.

In London the planners are trying to solve this kind of problem. They want to add the docks area and the adjoining marshland to London's living and working space. Some old docks have already been filled in or converted to other uses. New housing, schools, shopping areas, markets and open spaces are planned, together with new road and rail links.

But the success of the plan depends on whether industry and business can be attracted to the area. If the plan is carried through successfully, about 30 000 new jobs will be created. But the plan's development depends on what happens in Britain as a whole and throughout the world, what new industries are needed, how trade grows and whether money can be found to pay for the construction.

*A disused dock near the Tower of London has been made into a yacht marina*

# Index

This index will help you to look up things quickly.
The numbers refer to the pages of the book.

aircraft industry 29–30
air transport 86–7
alloys 29–30
aluminium 29–30
arable farms 64–7
automation 20

blast furnace 22

cheese-making 60
chemicals 14
civil engineering 28–9
clothing 35–40
coal 6, 7–8
coke 22
communications 90–92
computers 19–20
Concorde 30, 86
Confravision 92
contour lines 44
copper 29
cotton 36
county councils 46
cross-Channel transport 88

dairy farming 57–60
district councils 45
docks and terminals 93–5

earth-moving machinery 29
electrical power 10
electronics 18–19
environment and transport 89

Facsimile Transmission 92
farming 56–75
fossil fuels 6
fish farming 80
fishing industry 76–80
fire service, 46
fruit farming 71–4

gas, natural 9
glass-making 31–2

health services 46
hydro-electric power 11

knitting 39

iron and steel 21–9

man-made fibres 16–17, 35
map scales 42–4
maps: aircraft factories 30
  Britain 4
  car factories 26
  coalfields 7
  highland and lowland 54
  North Sea oil and gas fields 9
  roads and railways 5
  types of farming 75
  types of fish 76
  weather 53, 55
  wind and rainfall 54
market gardening 68–70
microprocessor 19
milk 59–60
motor car industry 25–6

North Sea gas and oil 9
North Sea transport 88
nuclear power stations 11

oil industry 9, 13–14

plastics 15, 16–17
polymers 15
polystyrene 16
postal services 90–91
potatoes 64–6
pottery 33–4
power stations 8, 10–11, 28
public library 46
Prestel 92

radiophone 92
railways 5, 83–5
refuse collection 47

remote control 19, 27
river pollution 49
roads, road transport 5, 82
robot assembly lines 26
rocking-float 12
RORO ships 88, 94

satellites 18, 55
seasons 51–2
sewage 50
sheep farming 61–6
ship building 27–8
silicon chip 18
silk 35
solar energy 12
spinning 38
steel 21, 23–9
sugar beet 67
sun 51–2

tailoring 40
telecommunications 91–2
telephones 91
Telex 91
thermoplastics 16, 17
thermosetting plastics 16, 17
tomatoes 68
transistors 18
transport 81–9
trawlers 77, 78–9

vegetables 64, 68–70
Viewdata 92

water supply 48–9
weather 53–5
weaving 39
wheat and barley 64, 67
wool 36

yarn, 36–7, 38